IMAGINE

SHANTA ACHARYA, born and educated in Cuttack, Odisha, won a scholarship to Oxford, where she was among the first batch of women admitted to Worcester College in 1979. A recipient of the Violet Vaughan Morgan Fellowship, she was awarded the Doctor of Philosophy for her work on Ralph Waldo Emerson. She was a visiting scholar in the Department of English and American Literature and Languages at Harvard University before joining Morgan Stanley in London. She worked in the asset management industry and has written extensively on the subject. The author of ten books, her publications range from poetry, literary criticism and fiction to finance. Founder of *Poetry in the House*, Shanta hosted a series of monthly poetry readings at Lauderdale House in London from 1996 to 2015. In addition to her philanthropic activities, she served twice on the board of trustees of the Po[illegible] in the UK.

Praise for Shanta Acharya

'It was the Danish physicist, Neils Bohr, who said that a great truth is a truth whose opposite is also a great truth. In poems rooted in the Upanishads, yet connecting through natural imagery with New England transcendentalism, Shanta Acharya summons courage to face such truths. It's hard to write "mystical" poetry these days, yet no other overall vision seems likely to prevent "the vulnerable plot of green", as she says, from being trampled by "frantic minds" not yet clear enough "to defend their humanity" by reconciling contradictions.' – **Anne Stevenson**

'Her clear vision has purged her writing of extraneous sentiment ... She cuts to the heart of things when, in one poem, she advises her readers to "discover in loneliness the continents of yourself".' – **Peter Porter**

'*Dreams That Spell the Light* is about voyaging through life, returning home and finding it changed, about confronting change and absences, about continents left behind, and a search for signs and "scripted dreams" that remain dreams. It is a book about secrets being locked up in sealed wells, and a "desire to fly free, not nailed to a mast". Shanta Acharya speaks of self-doubt and self-realization, of the cussedness of reality, of bonding with nature and of "love under starlight/brittle with frost and the sharp taste of blood".' – **Keki Daruwalla, *Ambit***

'Shanta Acharya's *Dreams That Spell the Light* philosophize on the spiritual intersection between locus and human existence, dancing with colour and luminosity, her poems beautiful and considered.' – **Jane Holland, *Poetry Review***

'A profound receptivity to the world distinguishes Shanta Acharya's new collection. Her acute eye and keen sense of form depict the outer world in vivid detail, invoking the inner world where human experience makes its reality. Here is a poet of much clarity of spirit and a wondrous gift for evoking place.' – **Penelope Shuttle**

'*Dreams That Spell the Light* is a book of wisdom and travel. The travel is troubled and wide, reflecting on the precariousness of life; the wisdom is drawn from a humane understanding of our place in the universe. But there is room for humour and pity and much close observation in these finely honed poems that work across cultures.' – **George Szirtes**

'Her poetry shows a rare combination of lyricism, intelligence, sagacity and a wicked sense of humour. She is not afraid to tackle large themes, to take on the abstract, metaphysical, spiritual or to use the idiom such themes demand. It is refreshing to find these qualities in such an engaging and individual voice.' – **Mimi Khalvati**

'Her poems have a melody and at the same time a vivid and down-to-earth quality which is really rare today. They are, so to speak, at home with themselves and not at all self-conscious. She often seems to be rescuing real poetry from the kinds of post-modern poeticism which are current today.' – **John Bayley**

'The poems in *Dreams That Spell the Light* are most unusual; bold in their spiritual sense, intense in their vision of landscape. It is a remarkable book which can revive a tired reader's vision, and alter their understanding of what poetry can do. I shall certainly think again about the scope of poetry – it's easy to settle for too little.' – **Alison Brackenbury**

'It is not often that poems like these, deeply rooted in personal experience, become such a sharply observed and cohesive sequence of "meditations", a poetry in which emotions are not merely recollected in tranquillity but are understood as part of an emerging pattern of perception about life's journey.' – **Dr Roger Pringle, Shakespeare Birthplace Trust**

'There aren't any trivial subjects in Acharya's work. What I like about her writing is the unpretentiousness, the integrity, the direct struggle with language to make it speak truly about real concerns.' – **R.V. Bailey, *Edinburgh Review***

'Shanta Acharya's is the true voice of the poet. She writes with poignancy and gentleness, with a mildness of manner behind which lurk wells of sad expressiveness and occasional acerbities. She controls her phrasing meticulously and invites the reader to return to her poems again and again to explore more hidden resonances and insights.' – **Alastair Niven**

'I like the uneasy tension that runs through the poems in *Dreams That Spell the Light*, the tension between home and abroad. One ends up asking, "What is home, and where is it?" Home is, at best, a state of mind. We carry our homes wherever we go. We build our homes in our poems. This is what Acharya has done, and she has done it without any melodrama.' – **Rajagopal Parthasarathy**

'...Out of the linguistic self-awareness come some convincingly accurate annotations of psycho-spiritual states ... Out of the tension between her two (or more) "languages" is created poetry of a very distinctive cast, which registers the poet's Indian origins without ever being merely exotic.' – **Glyn Pursglove, *The Swansea Review***

'Her beautifully evocative and lyrical poetry combines, effortlessly, the metaphysical and the quotidian, the political and the aesthetic.' – **Mark Mathuray, *Journal of Post-Colonial Writing***

'Shanta Acharya's poems are inspired by her emotional experiences, for which simple but convincing words, phrases and sound effects have been found. There is nothing artificial in her statements and choice of forms. The complex and profound are equally well expressed in her imagery.' – **Nissim Ezekiel**

'Shanta Acharya's latest volume gathers work from over two decades of vigorous and vivid writing, and adds a generous section of new poems. Acharya is concerned with the big, often painful subjects – death and loss, love's shortfalls, poverty and dispossession – but there are moments of humour and satire, and a rich aesthetic delight in the variousness of the world. Childhood memories and meditations in art galleries reveal a delight in colour and light. Acharya's poems are full of the pleasures of the unexpected.' – **Carol Rumens**

'Shanta Acharya has deep roots in two cultures – her country of birth and her country of adoption. Both are represented in this rich and varied collection of poetry, drawing from her previous collections. Her poems are a vivid and thoughtful way of exploring and reflecting on the world – on nature, on the world of art, and on the ironies of the human predicament. They also convey a deep spiritual interest, sometimes as a way of interrogating personal relationships, and reflecting on loss and longing. Shanta is very good at paying close attention to what she sees and conveying it in precise language. She is interested in often neglected corners of experience. She is not afraid of writing about horror, nor does she shirk from revealing vulnerability. But she is good at humour too, at seeing the ridiculous side of things, revealing a capacity for playfulness. In language that is accurate, spontaneous, and often witty, Shanta explores ways in which the modern individual can find a place in the world, having floated free of traditional supports. These are brave and thoughtful poems.' – **Carole Satyamurti**

'Shanta Acharya has an uncannily poetic way of relating to reality that is deeply Indian without being insular. Hers is a meditative spirit which however seldom abandons its interrogative scepticism that shapes its subtle politics. Her poetry quarrels with power in all its incarnations, divine and human, without ever being loud, and her emotional range is wide, from the pains of a girl's growing up in an unkind world to the pleasures of love and the abjectness of abandonment. She realizes that "knowing is all" and with it too that knowing is agony. Reading these poems together is like entering a house with many windows, each opening on a different landscape.' – **K. Satchidanandan**

'There is a stateliness and poise about Shanta Acharya's poetry that is remarkable. Her poetry grapples with life, the vicissitudes of fate, and much beyond. The variety of themes she explores and confronts is formidable – life, art, illusion, death. One observes the integrity of the poet as her true being emerges. This collection has a momentum of its own, the poetry inexorably moving towards an inner core. One puts down the volume with the feeling that one has come face to face with a true established poet.' – **Keki Daruwalla**

Imagine
New and Selected Poems

SHANTA ACHARYA

HarperCollins *Publishers* India

First published in India in 2017 by
HarperCollins *Publishers* India
Building 10, Tower A, 4th Floor, DLF Cyber City, Phase II,
Gurugram Haryana – 122002, India
www.harpercollins.co.in

P-ISBN: 978-93-5264-165-9
E-ISBN: 978-93-5264-166-6

2 4 6 8 10 9 7 5 3 1

Typeset in 10/13 Sabon Roman at
SÜRYA, New Delhi

Printed and bound at
MicroPrints India, New Delhi

For my mother
and in memory of my father

‘These fragments I have shored against my ruins…’

– T.S. Eliot

‘True singing’s a different breath. It has no choice,
Being nothing. A tremor in a god. A wind.’

– Rainer Maria Rilke

‘Thoughts take form with words,
but this daylight is beyond and before
thinking and imaging.’

– Jalāl ud-Dīn Muhammad Rūmī

CONTENTS

From Not This, Not That

For my parents and their parents

Wherefrom words turn back
Together with the mind, not having attained.

–Taittiriya Upanishad

The Soul is not this, it is not that.

–Brihadanyaka Upanishad

FAITH

There are things
you need not know
my mother once said
when I pricked my balloon
to discover what hid inside.

There are things
you need not know
my father once said
when I pricked my finger
to see how I bled.

There are things
you will fail to find
both my parents said
when I flew from their nest
to explore my brave new world.

WISDOM

The tree
stood massive
a fat grandparent

Laughing Buddha

Teaching young leaves
to jostle in the breeze
play with the sun.

CUCUMBER

Single
self-possessed
high on its stalk of green
the cucumber hangs

Untouchable

Signalling
wisdom
a Shiva-lingam dumbness
unprayable.

IN THE BEGINNING

In the beginning

Said the inverted tree
roots clutching the sun
leaves rotting in the mud

There was no sky.

The tree had a vision
before man razed the arches.
Did man know his own word?

DEATH

My words
shall fold the full-blown rose
to a bud unmuted by sin.

There shall be no flowering then.

And I shall lie
cold and wordless
pickled in a jar

Stillborn. Perfect like silence.

CREATION

As a child
I created friends
from songs I heard
stories I read
inside my head.

I learnt to be
richly content
with my elastic self
as I contained
crores of friends.

It seemed easy
to invent a creature
almost every day.
Nobody died
or suffered
in any maiming way.

So I gambolled
childhood away.
When I was taller,
virtually an adult,
I tiptoed into
archives of fiction.

Never realized
it was what
growing up
was all about
until I bled,
and mother
explained
what creation
and womanhood meant.

God does it every day –
I cried.
I too make life
in my own way,
creating
imaginary worlds
day after day.

UNSPOKEN

Once again resistant
flaming white icebergs

Emerge out of the ocean
in endless imbroglio.

The sunlight no longer
shines on anything immaculate.

I straighten the tippler in me
that stumbles, leaning across

The dark cellars of being
and will not stay still,

But watches for the moment alone
to torpedo these icebergs of silence.

THE VULNERABLE PLOT OF GREEN

Under our very different sun
there are no illusions
about the sacred realm of art,
the shaping power of the imagination,
nor for that matter the imperial self.

No longer sacrosanct
the vulnerable plot of green,
begging, *Please keep off the grass*
on rusting metal plates.

It is now criss-crossed
by the paths of haunted minds
frantic to defend
their humanity through art,
by means of a means,
the green season of the mind.

AGAINST THE WINDOW

Child, you practise well so young to stand
against the walls that limit your explorations.

Your face puckered up to break through the double-
glazing flattens into an illuminated Picasso print.

Cross-eyed, you search the face of an ubiquitous howler
while your lips frost the glass, chanting *Whoooo…*

Staring out as if the wind were playing hide-and-seek,
your whole attitude compact with the fiction.

DEAR BORN CHILD

Dear born child, you do not know,
with your sky so near, your world so free,
your vowels pouring as rain in summer
that men will fatten to murder and eat.

Now you do not know, innocent-eyed,
you too will wear the mark of Cain
or develop a cleft foot –
get used to this sort of thing.

You will metamorphose to a Kwakiutl Indian
if not a pure Swadeshi,
not fail to fall in a frenzy,
eat blood-soaked human flesh,
no matter your soul, hell or heaven.

A ritual mistake, dear born child,
may cost you more than you care
for men will tear you to pieces
and consume you like free fare.

A SENSE OF SECURITY

The creeper clung
to the rooftop in dismay
and terror of the lashing rain –
darkness of an unnatural afternoon.

The false ceiling dropped snakes
black sleek glossy
six inches of life
double-headed.

Feigning concern
I sprinkled kerosene
every time an emissary fell at my feet
expelled from its lofty lair.

I watched silently
the contortions of dying,
the sheer struggle for survival
when a match went up in flames.

From *Not This, Not That*

The fury of the storm
no longer frightened me,
when the dance of death was on
I felt secure as a god.

CALIGULA

I was only learning to accept
what I could not alter
in a lifetime of abominable power –

Caligula's ghost muttered
inarticulate
to the raving winds of change.

Emperors all
secretly quaked with fear
of losing their sacred power.

In the mountains streams untamed
rushed down like children
bursting out of closed classrooms.

The wind among the shadows of trees
chased the spangles of sunshine in between.

Into the plains the river veered
like a god carving its own course.

Who dare challenge a god's intractable voice
swollen like a tyrant?

Caligula did.
And in his madness understood
the lonely god in him.

LIFE AND DREAMS

No longer do I weigh the happiness
of life with any measure of dreams.

As one dream in its course foundered,
hydra-like another was engendered.

Phoenix-like dreams were born,
sustaining life's panoramic illusion.

In between dreams I survived
awake hungry alone,
adjusting my philosophy to my dreams
as life kept stretching reality at its seams –

the pattern of my dream-jacket
woven sparingly with meagre originality
though laced grandly with gaudy ribbons of reality.

Perhaps I do not have the stomach to dream,
imagine butterflies grow into killer bees.

Dreams are meant to help me live,
not turn into nightmares, usurp my peace.

An overdose of reality can maim or blind,
adversity is not always a booster for the mind.

Crippled by false gods, unable to cherish
miracles that transform lives, I let the rain
caress my skin, skim the salt in tears moistening
my lips, no longer ask why caged birds sing.

IN THE JAGANNATH TEMPLE

Under the shamiana of a tree
in the haunting twilight
of the temple precincts in Puri
sits a leper in lotus pose –
Jagannath centred in his self.

His features reflected in the light
from the passing lamps of pilgrims
haunt the ambience of prayers,
the accompaniment of temple bells
to the priests' blowing conch shells.

Grotesque anonymity fascinates –
the imagination similarly crippled
awaits the toss of a coined idea
to sustain its existence –

Jagannath swami, prabhu antaryami...
mouth holes froth praises to his maker
as gods emerge out of decrepitude.

IF ONLY I WERE

The chameleon wind blowing over
the rugged ranges of the Himalayas.

A tree in full regalia of autumn
on a peacock-blue lake in Vermont.

A bee upon a raft of sunlight
in the gardens of this nurturing earth.

A coral formation along the Great Barrier Reef.
The robe of the night sky filigreed with stars.

A jugalbandi raga at dawn
of sitar and shehnai, sarangi and tabla.

A wild flower greeting the weary
explorer in some forgotten desert.

A rainbow poised over the Iguacu Falls
chanting, *make me always the same as I am now.*

If only I were Mother Teresa's eyes
watching over a sick, sleeping child.

A dream come true in the warm smiles
of all the children in our world.

Hands that heal, mend what is broken,
truth that frees the innocent, falsely accused.

From *Not This, Not That*

The biting, trusting grip of a new-
born child at the mother's breast.

The voices of poets, thinkers, artists, the words
of inspiration in the struggle of our daily lives.

DAY OF RECKONING

I knew it would arrive one day
possibly in the guise of just another day,
never revealing its purpose or plan
nor suggesting what it was supposed to mean.
It was not a rendezvous I could prepare for.

Life was stronger than myself, I acknowledge.
Things I valued had been stripped away
by sudden manoeuvres – love, poetry, freedom
I'd treasured as sunlight or a breath of fresh air.

Whatever I had grown accustomed to expect
was perpetually beyond mine to have or cherish.
These exquisite toys were loaned to me for moments,
to be renounced without notice as if that was a gift.
Granted that change is the only steady state.

Sisyphus-like I am cursed with futile labour,
eternally swapping my days for some promised nirvana.
Having discarded all my transient toys, I wait alone
the coming of my day of reckoning. Preparedness is all.

Learning to live, amid uncertainties, with grace and faith,
even an element of charity. Doubting, but not sceptical.
Possessing, yet prepared to relinquish all,
if need be, in the right spirit, no remorse, no loss.
Not presuming nor damning, I pretend not to prepare at all.

BELSHAZZAR'S FEAST

(After the painting by Rembrandt in the National Gallery, London)

In the Dutch room amid Rembrandt's paintings,
I sit sharing my reflections with myself –
my woollen jacket no comparison with Belshazzar's
mantle of ermine studded with jewels,
his silk turban, white and resplendent,
crowning his distracted gaze.

The room acquires the aura of a court in session,
members of the jury appear unmoved,
floating like creatures treading on the moon.
The wooden bench, the murmuring crowd,
the parched sensation in my throat,
deeper rumblings in my stomach,
tired eyes and cold feet, a bone marrow fatigue
alienates me from the artistic feat.

The haloed hand, the writing on the wall,
offer unexpected food for thought.
Mene Mene Tekal Upharsin. You have been
weighed in the balance and found wanting.
Belshazzar's face aghast with such revelation!
Do not despair, one was saved; do not presume, one was damned.

I close my eyes thinking of god mercifully
adjusting the divine scales in my favour –
myself poised on one side, insubstantial;
my burden of sins on the other, weighing down
heavy, leaving me quite unbalanced.

So god kept adding extra weights of suffering
to help me overcome my *unbearable lightness of being*
like an ingenious doctor shrewdly intent
on restoring me to life by increasing daily
the bitter pills of my life in self-exile.

I had a vision of grace reconciling me
to myself, to see me poised and not wanting.

You may have mistaken my strength, dear God
to emerge from your gift of suffering balanced.

CUPID COMPLAINING TO VENUS

(After the painting by Lucas Cranach, the Elder, in the National Gallery, London)

Cupid's cherubic limbs
while stealing honey
have been stung by bees,
the honeycomb still in his hand.

Venus, in reply to Cupid's passionate complaint,
reckons that such is the reward of love –
there is no ecstasy without agony.
That was Eve's curse and Adam's fate.

The pursuit of pleasure in love is in vain,
love walks hand-in-hand with pain.
Be wary Cupid where your truant arrows aim.

Is that the reason Krishna counselled
a grief-stricken Arjuna, blinded like Cupid
by the contrary passions of his heart
driving him crazy, tearing him apart
to be like a lotus in a pond –
unsoiled, unattached?

I wonder if that is what Krishna meant...

THE POSTER STICKER

In the narrow lanes of Cuttack
poverty secures for itself an eminence.

The wayside urchin hauls up a huge
colourful poster of Bombay's film stars
who return to him in his dreams each night,
offering escape from the drudgery of his life.

He is rich and famous like Amitabh Bachchan,
young and dashing like Hrithik Roshan.
Beautiful girls chase him, money is no constraint.
He is the local hero by popular consent.

His dreams are so real, he can feel them
like the silver coins that are the sole reward
of his endless labours, day after day.

Short-changed, his Aishwarya slips
through cracked sheets of posters,
mocking his lack of opportunity in such matters.

Desperately holding on to his dreams
as a talisman, he returns to hoist his nightmare
newly printed on the pissed walls of this city.

BUS RIDE TO CHAR MINAR

Cramped in a corner
I ride a bus to Char Minar.
Bursting bodies press on me
as strangeness begs familiarity
in sharing a hard, narrow seat.

I feel the soft, wrinkled skin
of an old Hyderabadi begum
leaning to the window for fresh air,
gasping curses on Allah for her plight.

The mother with child at her breast
squats near my feet, quite content.
Two little dirty hands tug innocently
the edge of my crumpled shawl.

Before I mingle again
in the crowd of Char Minar,
two sunken eyes offer me
eternity in a begging bowl,
promising me a reserved seat
in the crowded bus to heaven
provided I pay the commission.

FEVER IN DIWALI

Pious neighbours celebrated Diwali
with neat rows of oil lamps
promising the destruction of evil.

My fever flew fast through the coil of night,
setting ablaze the desolate sky
like a child conspiring with confetti stars.

Harassed doctors came with tablets,
magic, miniature moons
with syrup in exorcist cups, a hermetic brew.

While the snake-charmer's fluted thermometer
grinned its flinted fangs wider and wider,
I ate moons and laughed at stars.

My limbs could've even danced a few steps to appease
evil with the grace of lightning in a storm-ripped sky
like blue-throated Shiva with snakes in red matted hair.

White sheeted, I lay still
like an Indian monkey in summer.

GANESH PUJA

A god sits alone
flushed in artificial neon lights,
red-blue-yellow-green chasing each other.

The fragrance of burnt-out joss sticks,
incense and oil lamp wicks mingle
with the smell of yesterday's flowers.
A god is left contemplating the world.

The puja ceremoniously done
the worshippers leave, one by one.
Even the priest retires to his daily chores.

I shall sit with you
lonely boy with the elephant trunk,
recreating myths
the years have forgotten to share with us.

I sit alone with a god alone
flushed in artificial neon lights,
red-blue-yellow-green chasing each other.

DUSSEHRA IN CUTTACK

For nine nights and ten days
        it was the festival of Dussehra.
Durga puja began with father
        tuning in to Radio Calcutta –
Akashvani, the voice from heaven –
        at dawn, hypnotic.
The chanting of the Mahamantras
        lulled me gently back to sleep.

The days were filled with laughter and games.
    Our family home resonated with voices
of relatives and friends, their relatives and friends –
    generations milling about, gossiping.
It was open house with mother in the kitchen
    and father in the sitting room.
The servants in their puja attire were keen to please,
    it was the season for gifts and bakshish.

The aroma of pulav and curries, chutneys and sweets
    competed with the fragrances of flowers,
joss sticks and the smell of diyas burning.
    This, our thanksgiving – the ritual
of preparing and sharing a sumptuous feast
    to welcome the Goddess Durga
into our heart and home –
    our gratitude for her limitless grace.

The evening promenade in the streets
    to the accompaniment of song and dance –
music wild with self-abandonment,
    resembling a rich tapestry of dreams –
promised a spectacle of life with its unceasing variety.

Enthroned on a rickshaw open wide to the skies,
    not in purdah in grandfather's Chevy
like my older female relatives, I wait impatiently
    a ride to the best show in town!
Aged about five and a half,
    I could've climbed over the moon
as our rickshaw-walla cycled us off crazily
    to worship the Durga images in town.

Sometimes we got off our burnished pedestal
to cast a more discerning look –
me, perched on my uncle's shoulders
for a safe and unrestricted view.
The face of Durga spearing the demon Mahisha
was calm, filled with serenity.
Her fish-shaped eyes, black and beautiful
shone from within, lit by a smile.

Back at home I re-enacted
our adventure into this land of myths,
my choreography inspired by
deep admiration for such a sublime woman –
my head filled with fantastic figures,
some with her tongue sticking out
in shame and surprise when discovered
with her foot placed firmly on
her husband's chest, a garland of skulls
enhancing her terrible beauty.

Durga-Kali's collection of toys meant
she was well-prepared for war or peace.
That was no easy act to surpass,
with her ten arms, three eyes,
a huge pet tiger to ride upon,
bejewelled like a bride.
Transformed by adoration,
a dancer in this dance of illusion,
sleep-laden, I drifted in a trance
into a world of demons and shining goddesses.

The immersion ceremony was the final act
on the banks of the ancient Mahanadi –
an annual mela, signifying yoga,
the connection between all things.
Drums beat in a rising rhythm,
the priests' chants gathered momentum,
hawkers advertised their wares
with greater frenzy as the crowd thickened.

The heat and light, sweat and dust,
smells, sounds and colours churned
into a crescendo of saffron, blurring the senses.
The vermillion sun was poised on the horizon
like a rich lady looking down upon us
through orange-filtered opera-glasses.

On the dusky banks of this majestic river
the grand spectacle of Dussehra is over –
dust to dust will return,
Durga and her cortege will melt
in the river that will not cease to flow
undisturbed like the gods, goddesses, demons
carried away after last year's celebrations.

Hanging on to my brother's arm for company,
I count the stars and the human pyres
burning in the distant crematorium.
The curtain descends on us mortals
as we prepare for our tired journey home.

THE NIGHT OF SHIVA

I

In my top-floor maisonette
solitary in Highgate
on Shivaratri I celebrate
Shiva's commemoration night,
reading ancient Hindu folklore,
fasting on a feast of fruits
from foreign shores –
pineapples, pomegranates, plums,
kiwi-fruits, mandarins, dates –
as I chant *Om Namah Shivayam*
magic formula for the alchemy
of sins into nirvana,
keeping vigil for a god
whose face had etched
itself into my tabernacle
memory as a curious child
one summer afternoon
a golden time of discovery
in a sprawling bungalow
on the banks of Mahanadi
when the world was revealed
framed in a poster
not of an Indian film star
but a face to remember
to love and cherish
though not to obey –
my Lord Shiva.

II

My restless mind wanders back
to a moonless night in Bhubaneswar –
home of gods, city of temples
of exquisite beauty and mosaic history –
where I dissolve like the first rains
of the monsoon into the parched earth.

I remember the night of Shiva
with father in crisp, white dhoti
and tussar Punjabi shirt.
Mother in yards of peacock-
throated pasapalli silk, changing colour
with the night's chameleon lights –
elephants, lotuses, lions, mandalas,
shielding her from evil eyes,
mantra woven into the Orissi fabric.
My brothers more modern in jeans,
T-shirts, Seiko watches, Nike shoes.

III

To the temple of Shiva we flocked
like lost sheep in search of our shepherd.
Lingaraja –
shrine dedicated to the face of my dreams
though worshipped by millions in the image
of a munificent phallus erect on a yoni.

Strange indeed are the ways of our gods,
representations of our perception of It –
not unlike positions listed in the Kama Sutra.
In all the temples of Shiva tonight
women will kiss the lingam without shame or thought.

Contraception, pills, IUDs, condoms –
unfamiliar words we half heard accidentally
when the adults thought it safe to speak freely.

AIDS or HIV had not yet marked
our fragile, adolescent memory.

We had not accounted for nature's inebriety,
not in the course of our childhood piety –
gay, lesbian, homosexual, bisexual,
heterosexual, transgender, hermaphrodite
had not quite entered our vocabulary.

Perhaps I will thank Lord Shiva tonight
for the gift of innocence and our naïveté.

IV

Joining the pilgrims from neighbouring villages,
we lighted rows of earthen lamps
rich with camphor and incense –
offered flowers, coconuts, silver coins, prayers
for the many miracles to transform our lives.

We waited for the high priest's communion,
for him to draw a halo round our heads,
his arati blessing us, the rice and the tulsi
nestling in the curls of our thick, black hair
as he gave us each the holy vermillion
on a tender bel-patri, green as memory.

Chanting Shiva's names, hundreds of them,
he offered us the diya, the holy flame,
fresh sandalwood paste for our foreheads
and water from Ganga in a bronze chalice.
I closed my eyes, palms folded in prayer
as I felt the sandalwood paste tighten my skin.

Anchored in the middle of a bubbling vulva-like geyser –
into whose vortex the priests poured offerings
of coconuts, rice, milk and honey, garlands of flowers,
miniature snakes of gold and silver,
bananas gone rusty brown, limp like deflated members –
stood solid in stone the object of our worship.

Bare-footed in sanctified mud, ooze and slime,
we walked like seasoned explorers on a slippery climb,
swaying to the rhythm of the divine temenos
situated in the cave-womb lit with a circle of lamps
of hope and despair, faith and forgiveness.

Blessed and blessing, we joined the revellers
cheering the novice, clambering up to the temple-pinnacle
like the monkey-god, Hanuman. The beacon of glory
beckoning all to participate in Shiva's feast.

V

On this night of our Mahadeva –
the creator of Brahma-Vishnu-Indra,
the essence It-Self whom all worship –
those who can focus their thoughts on Shiva
can achieve knowledge and powers divine.

The temple dancers performed tandava nrutya,
depicting how the master of flux,
the end and the beginning of all things,
danced his steps of destruction and regeneration –

how Shiva swallowed the poison of our world
and bottled it in his throat for our benefit,
holding the mighty Ganga in his matted locks.
We gleaned how Ganesha acquired his elephant's head.

While myths and legends stretched our notions of humanity,
the Atman revealed itself to be not this, nor that.

VI

It would be a thousand blessings
to meet you, auspicious One, in Mount Kailash
with Parvati, Ganesha and Kartikeya.

That journey I hope to make before my time is up.
Tonight I'll settle for a glimpse of you
in any place you care to visit in London.

With your dreadlocked hair,
tiger-skin mini-skirt pinned in place
by snakes coiled tight round your body,
your third eye shining like a nebula –
drum in one hand, trishul in the other,
your rhythmic dance would be quite an ethnic
performance par excellence with Parvati
breakdancing round Trafalgar Square,
looking chic in her garland of human heads.

VII

If you decide to answer my prayer,
stop for a moment your
centuries of meditation,
I will be waiting here
patiently, keeping my solitary
vigil for your coming.

Om Namah Shivayam.

The phone rings
and I hear a strange voice say:
This is Shiva speaking…

From Numbering Our Days' Illusions

For my friends

As the sun, the eye of the whole world,
Is not sullied by the external faults of the eyes.

–Katha Upanishad

Depart passionless through the door of the sun.

–Mundaka Upanishad

AFTER GREAT STRUGGLE

After great struggle
descends
an alternative calm.
The mind's swirling sky
now emptied of its thoughts in snowstorm.

Wrapped up like Trappist monks
the trees preserve an immaculate silence.

The cold wind shakes
this proud stillness

into crumbling flakes,
mercilessly
smiling at the helpless struggle

to keep up appearances at all costs.

Strange faces
sheathed
move in these streets

wanting a more direct relation with the sun.

SILENCE

With the eloquence of figurines on Konarka,
the inscrutable dialogue of rainbows
conversing with heaven in one language
and the horizon in others, your silence speaks.

I too prefer the silence of the moon,
the silence of the inmates of heaven's harem,
the voluptuous stars.

Smiling at the fragmentary utterances of men,
memory only creates words out of memory,
beguiling us with its repertoire of tricks.

If love chooses to be silent as eternity is,
will it signify anything else?

There is more poetry in a kiss
than in all the words that trade between us.

ARRANGED MARRIAGE

The bridegroom's profile
refracted through her purdah
of tears unused to the violence
of iconoclasm dressed as tradition.

That moment's reappraisal
warned her to faithlessness,
discard old ways for new,
worship new gods and shoes.

She was the arrow then
that darted forth from
the taut bow of culture into
the flaming pyre, proclaiming
impossible union with a stranger.

Love will rise like a phoenix, they said,
friendship will follow with the children of god.
But first one has to be turned inside out.

HONEYMOON

Afloat on a raft towed by dreams
we gushed down a wild river's course
with nothing much to hold on to
save perhaps the stars in our eyes.
Neither of us saw the storm
gathering in the horizon
that broke our homely raft in two.
With closed eyes you drank deep the honey
and left me with the cold platter of a moon.

THE DARK HOURS

I shun your shadow
as the wailing of dogs.

In the dark hours
blind flapping of wings,
the air fluttering wildly
with a haphazard moth's naïveté
caught in the jaws of a lizard.

You eclipsed my sun
in your vast shadow,
cutting down my sunflower world
with your rapier fingers.

Heaped on the floor I lay
discoloured,
your cudgelled blows of deceit
convulsing:

Feeling deep the deer
against hound in my marrow.

Look stranger,
you can hurt no longer.
The dappled moth escaped
trembling
waltz-winged.

Sometimes towards sunset
I watch the embers fade
my anger to indifference.

The moth shall grow wings to fly.
The sun shall open my sky.

FACE OF BETRAYAL

Tonight the storm howls my words back,
dead, mutilated like corpses.

Flashing lightning smiles of torture at me –
a mad scorpion lashing
my truth thunders in a black pall of falsehood.

Pointing leprous fingers of contempt,
they screech with the frightened owl.

I have seen the face of betrayal,
cold, unfamiliar –
the glorious sunset fading.

PROMISE

Around the walls
of an ancient temple
you led me in rapture
carving words
seven unredeemable times.

Your words
like the full-throated chant
of the Buddhist monks in prayer
rose to an immaculate crescendo
showering me
with a spring harvest of silence.

NUMBERING OUR DAYS' ILLUSIONS

Your flowers stand back in my bottle vase
precious like these hypocritical days
that depart silent full of contempt,
offering a majestic ruse of vision.

I search for words on bright yellow
walls of sunlight that stand between us
every morning patiently watching
our shadows flow into each other.

We grow with the sun,
numbering our days' illusions.

A MOMENT'S OCCUPATION

Spread out alive as a river on arid soil,
I wish to be perfectly empty,
lie with my eyes turned upwards
in evacuation of all desires.

Suddenly, I am pitched into a whirlpool,
mounted on sense, arched in ecstasy,
churned in the trill of a moment's freedom.

In some distant angle
the sun bends the light on my vision
beyond a moment's occupation.

THE CHOICE

I

My mind imagining itself
a shaft of sunlight
refracted in your medium.

With my several selves
I folded myself into your body
content to be a colourful crowd,
celebrating in your prismatic streets
for a frail moment only.

I never begged eternity or your soul,
only the choice to be free –
a promise given at the beginning of time
to let the sunlight play in our streets.

II

This present fiction is of my mind.
A familiar pain trails the mind's creations
released in what-might-have been.

Realigning forces, I emerge the same,
out of myself, endlessly emerging
to surprise your fragmented selves
though destined to miss you.

My body, cold and critical,
stirs to draw the curtain
and let the sunlight stream in.

TOO MEAGRE

Too meagre it was to die for you,
letting myself down in such a paltry fashion.

It would have proved nothing,
living is the hardest miracle.

You always knew it was no longer possible –
beyond the betrayal, dying is a trifle,
no longer an art to be perfected.
That has been mastered before.

Life is a shaft of sunlight
that does not enter my room anymore.

It is costlier, I must confess
since passion through contracting breath
heaved the centre of my days with you.

I offer you this for it includes
the deaths without the dying,
without the respite to be dead
nor breathe the pretence of death.

FACING THE SUN

Dying roots facing the sun
endure a felled-tree dumbness
long after your words struck the axe
in heaving me out of my centre.

My leaves clutching the earth
hear the hooves of words retreating.

I never anticipated this spoliation
from the elusive encounters of our knowing
that admitted only a moment's tethering.

You too never reckoned such leafing,
recompense shimmering green in the sun,
before you began this felling.

Here, then my necessary defoliation
to overcome a majestic ruse of vision –
the disjointed centaur of your stance,
now familiar your routes of escape.

Rising among the shadows of your words
are shapes that you keep slaying until
your words are no longer echoes travelling.

This uprooted-tree ambience once breathed
my unspoken words spangle the sun.

SOMETIMES

People change, and smile: but the agony abides.

–T.S. Eliot

I

Sometimes when the nights are long
and my thoughts empty,
full of the silence of words
never meant to be spoken,
I know in the darkness
between us nothing can be over.

I look through the curtains
for the stars lest they disappear
in this torpid air of disaffection.

Sometimes when I am
completely at peace with myself
wrapped in bed en route to my dreams,
I know there wasn't anything we could do.

I walk past all our celebrated ways of knowing
into my innermost temple where you sit.
I confess to you how broken I am,
how frail these hours without you.

II

Sometimes in my sleep I wake up howling,
dreaming I am drowning
in some unknown seas, of wars
strangely enough in our streets,
and my mother near the stained-glass window,
her thoughts incandescent in silence –
my tears seek only your touch.

I search for you in these lingering hours,
remembering how we embraced the time you said:

This is the most permanent thing in the world.
I emerged pure as the ritual.

III

You always preferred silence,
refraining from words to fill me
with your infinite loneliness.

At a touch of your hands a whole new
view of the world passed into my mind.

It is not as if now you are silent
even though I may pretend it to be so.

Your absence hurts me like your words
that having lived in this room know
just how I poised as a wave ready
to break on your eager shores.

IV

Sometimes you loved me too
with all your loneliness, your silence.

With the gift of this silence
I carve these words for you.

Our relationship wanted not the intensity
but a certain fullness of expression.

There is no use in trying to examine
such things later, none of us can retreat in time.

Every new relation is a new word
struggling against silences to come.

I no longer hope against hope for your return,
nor am I certain this spring's flowers
will be less fragrant without you.

I am not even sad my love could not contain you.

If you were to come back to me,
I would quicken each pulse in you
and from freedom set you free.

V

Sometimes when I think I had
given you all, yet you walked away
full of me, I breathe solitude none can share.

Knowing it not, whatever one desires
one is. Knowing is all.

FORGETTING

Forgetting is like wintering here,
a lonely preoccupation.

The assiduity of mists
learning to balance
on moving shadows of sunshine
is what tired eyelids close upon.

Awareness is restful
though seeing is fatiguing.

Squinting of eyes dazzled
by light on snowscape is merciful.
Seeing, though free, is dear to negotiate.

The sunshine is excitable too,
forgetting it is white winter still,
offering in its shafts golden amnesia.

LOVE GAME

When two individuals meet
and the chemistry is right
for friendship and love and more,
whatever the final score,
they consent to play a complex game
with two sets of jigsaw puzzles
of each other's identity
except the pieces are all part
of the other's chameleon personality
and one is expected to assemble
an image of the other
with one's capacity to feel,
to sense one's way to the other
like a game of chess being played
by the imagination alone,
and the game is not to checkmate
your partner but to anticipate
every word, action and thought,
picking fragments that fit into place,
the pieces finally beginning to make sense.

In their efforts to identify what they love,
two friends help create the lover in the other.
Often the essence is discarded or simply lost
for one cannot construct the full image ever.
It is a process of intuitive selection
better known as self-preservation.
So when I create you, I create what I love.
The rest I leave as excess baggage in life's journey,
hoping that life will not compel me later
to put all of a lifetime's pieces together.

From *Numbering Our Days' Illusions*

I may not have the courage or the desire
to take a good look at all of myself or you.

If I can create as complete a picture of you
(knowing that time is the best artist of all)
and you attempt to do the same of me
with a lot of help from each other,
we stand a pretty good chance of never
having to fall out of love with each other.
That's why I'm content to let us take a bit longer
than is customary in affairs of the heart
to get our jigsaw puzzle fit right from the start.

IT IS

It is not when you are coming to meet me
with my eyes anxiously waiting to cast their net in yours,
my body pitching all the colours of your mind
arched in ache like a quivering rainbow taut
across your skies of casual encounters.

It is when I am turning away alone,
tired not with what you give, but what you deny
for the lack of which are we both unredeemable.

No longer grappling with the inane art
of naming things and deconstructing them,
only being in one corner of consciousness, subliminal,
we will perhaps discover that love is.
I am not even sure that is the name.

HAVING SETTLED MYSELF

People wish to be settled; only as far as they are unsettled is there any hope for them.

–Ralph Waldo Emerson

Having settled myself
into this mutual infidelity,
concert appears not
the sole valency of strength.

Did you think it strange
that we should be devoured
by a lie that spreads through
our words and smiles?

Truth comes in strokes of pain.
We compose in vain the broken refrain
of a song no longer sung from the heart.

Living consists in
procuring temporary anodyne.

Having mastered the reflexes
of an inner writhing,
knowing we could never pitch the abyss,
our saturnalia is destitution of faith.

In mutual recrimination
we align in our confession,
irreversible this slow sclerosis of breath.

At intervals I stop to scorn
my own paltry performance –
weary of charades and artefacts
though recognizing the need for all that.

I can no longer live disinherited
in your gilded world
of convertible bonds and champagne.

It does not take much to keep intact
one's integrity. That much I can state
for a fact, having settled myself into this and that.

NO LONGER DO I FRAME MYSELF

No longer do I frame myself in mirrors.
It is not as if I have finally gone beyond self-
adoration, nor is it that the glass cracks across
and my image aborts in a familiar nemesis.

It's only an emptiness whose depths disturb
the smooth surfaces of reality.

Soon you will be aware of absences,
I whisper to the mirror
with receding memories of other presences
that grew beside me like trees,
colourless, dead with blighted leaves.

The branches mock my featurelessness.
Strange greeting for having accomplished
the ultimate miracle – complete effacement of self.

Steeled with the sheen of a glassy light
the mirror continues with nonchalance its illusions.

Perfect, a white pillar of light,
I now float across mirrors
that once dared to catch me in multiple images.

NOT ONE OF THE MYTHS

Not one of the myths we make
will outlast the muting of our breath.

What comes and goes in silence
represents time's landscape of self.

So long estranged from myself,
I have created an illusion –

carefully camouflaged
to welcome our re-entrance.

It is like passing from the object
to its unredeemable shadow.

Like leaping off the canvas of a painting
into the gallery of free spectators –

only to dread that moment of return
to another image that would recapture us.

A plastic version of all that passed among us
or others who unknowingly resembled us.

The imageless wind is the appropriate conception,
projecting the naked self, the final relation.

There arrives a time when the fiction is a mirror
image of itself, a thing final in itself.

Unable to discern between illusion and creation,
we have stopped revolving in self-abnegation.

From *Numbering Our Days' Illusions*

After the wind has gathered its unique composure
and we breathe deeply the pure, fulfilling air,

our halcyon gestures resurrect words from silence
like conjurors revelling in tricks and games.

The myths dissolve in the silence that guts
our ineffectual, self-mutilating words.

ABSENCE

Spread against the damask-rose sky
my thoughts fly home,
white cranes into the sunset.

They have travelled in echelons
to melt into the twilight,
flaming satis in regal poise.

In your absence this sunset
is a funeral of dream petals,
a pyre stoked up with volatile promises.

HINDU WOMEN

In the Hindu niche of my heroines' gallery
hang some exclusive miniature portraits,
top girls worshipped in their country.

Savitri is one whose puja is done by my mother,
paying homage to the Sati's indisputable power
in renegotiating the lease on the life of her husband
from repossession by Yama to populate his land.

Then, there is Sita's story to marvel upon.
After twelve years in exile from home and throne,
not to mention the ordeal of being courted by ten-faced Ravana,
Sita was expected to defend her chastity
in a trial by fire as decreed by some committee.
Much too embarrassed by her own husband and king, Rama,
she prayed for the earth to protect her honour.

Miraculously, Mother Earth did rise to the occasion,
sheltering Sita from the ignominy of such purification.
Imagine Sita's expression as she bowed out in style –
relief, surprise, pride, sorrow, loss, vindication –
all captured in her face, struggling for domination.

Draupadi, a free spirit, chose Arjuna in a swayamvara
and unwittingly acquired five husbands to protect her.
So she thought until pawned away by Yudhishtira
in a drunken game of dice loaded with their lost honour.
Humiliated in public she escaped being stripped naked
by the shameless Kauravas, sheathed in her magical sari.

Parvati, also called Durga, is both Kali and Gauri.
She has a thousand names and incarnations –
being wedded to Shiva, the creator–preserver–destroyer
of the universe, can make anyone schizophrenic.
No wonder she needs multiple personalities
to mix and match with every crises.

As Kali she is formidable in her garland
woven from her victim's heads –
as Durga she smiles on all creatures
in a gesture of sublime apotheosis.

Radha with Krishna remain at the centre
of this mandala with their song and dance,
their legendary love and romance.

Lakshmi and Saraswati, supreme goddesses –
Lakshmi of virtue, purity, wealth and success,
Saraswati of knowledge and art, the quintessence
of being – reach out to my inner recess.

Merging into one versatile deity,
they urge me to celebrate life's infinite variety,
steadying my passage through an uncertain world.

RESIGNED

Naked I came
reduced to my alphabets,
a tree trying to be a seedling,
confessing all
through shifts in our stances of embracing,
twitching of finger-ends and eyes crossing.
Having been failed by all –
all my words and yours, our promises,
I resigned to be dumb and unmoved,
let what is being be.

LOOSE TALK

You can hold your peace all on your own
if you can learn to hold your tongue.
And, if anything is not to your liking, it is best
to take the name of the Lord, *Hari Om*,
for that is not in vain – with some such words
my tongue-tied grandmother gifted away
the treasures of her wisdom to her daughter.

My mother, sharing her legacy, taught me yoga –
how to bend my body like a bow, raise it like a snake,
roar like a lion, stretch my tongue as far as my nose.
I encouraged my mother to loosen her tongue,
it was her story I yearned to hear
in her words, unfurling like the national flag
on Independence Day to the anthem we sang together.

My mother tongue is Oriya –
mysterious as Chilika, lyrical as Konarka.
I grew up in English, inhabiting words
from a distant island that took me home.
How can I keep my worlds apart,
cast away my runaway tongue?

Critics like ruthless children pelted my forked-
tongue which had not learnt to rattle.
In a world devoid of plain speak I sought
remedy from my goddesses, companions
to the muses: Hiss, child hiss!
They whispered their secret syllables,
and I graduated from an obedient stutter
to shedding my shame, singing my song.

From *Numbering Our Days' Illusions*

With tongues of fire I speak –
for grandmothers and mothers in silent revolt,
for daughters and sisters striving to be heard –
lending my voice, sharing our story.

Drunk with the variousness of the world,
I am mistress of my tongue,
kavita flows from my fingertips –

soaring high as a hawk, gentle as tortoise,
knowing nothing, everything – laughing buddhas,
auroras dancing to the music of the universe,
my verse bitter neem, divine nectar,
deep as thought, brief as a moment,
an epic Himalayan avalanche,
submarine volcanoes lighting a ring of fire.

Crooked as truth, I create pearls of wisdom
with years of polishing, coming full circle
to my grandmother's home-truths –
balancing a world of words in my mouth.

MEDITATION IN A BATHTUB

Condensation on the mirror
wipes me out of my orbit.

The rising steam of illusions
mould on the attic's ceiling.

Reflections blur the world escalated
with thoughts' unredeemable patterns.

I, Lady Narcissus,
seek only the unperturbed surface,
a clean, white, deadly mirror.

A GIDDY MANNEQUIN

A giddy mannequin discreetly naked
I pose for you in a glass cage,
out of your reach, perfect and undefiled.

I learnt the use of façades
when you began destroying my porcelain dolls
so long treasured behind the purdah of myself.

Dead images, my mirrors in pieces,
I strive to escape continually
the incarnation of my several selves
strewn casually over our encounters in time.

They glisten into life mocking me at multiple angles
as I puppet-dance to your discordant tunes.
I pretend not to take notice of such things.

Even this discerning unconcern
I stole from your eyes, unaware,
perfected to an art of survival

As you in perpetual ambush
prefer to remove your glasses
before you come forward to splinter mine.

I have nothing to be sad about
as our images crackle and drag.

My body remains silent and complete,
a giddy mannequin discreetly naked.

ON REMEMBERING A NAME

She would talk a little to herself as she combed her hair,
Repeating his name with its patient syllables,
Never forgetting him that kept coming constantly so near.

–Wallace Stevens

Is it your name that approaches
without you, interminable adventurer?

There is always something moving
in the memory of your name.

I can even preserve my footsteps
within its sacred space.

Your name is not to be profaned
when I hold durbar of all my selves.

The repeating of your name focuses
the edges of my blurred and frayed self.

The syllables in orchestral shapes
appear tenderly gleaning my days.

It is a useful swastika at the precipice of memory,
whirling me straight into the eye of my loss.

DAUGHTERS AND LOVERS

I

Cordelia could not heave her true heart into her
mouth, even for her fond and foolish father.

Lear had loved her most, yet in a moment's
reversal disowned her without any dowry,
without his grace, his love, his benison,
becoming himself the natural fool of fortune.

He went to night school in the storm on a heath
with a fool, a follower, and a madman.
Lear soon learnt: *Is man no more than this?*
A poor, bare, forked animal as thou art?

But worse was still to come
for Lear was King Lear still:
I am a very foolish fond old man.

Carrying his dead daughter in his arms,
his poor fool hanged, fools both of fate,
fools of the gods of human nature.

Like a tired child on stage,
Lear went to sleep with Cordelia in his arms.

II

Enter Hamlet musing to himself:
To be, or not to be – that is the question...

Ophelia appears thinking that Hamlet's love
for her is the reason for his distraction.

In two simple sentences he confirms her suspicion –
I did love you once. And then, *I loved you not.*

His solution for her was meant sincerely:
Get thee to a nunnery,
Why wouldst thou be a breeder of sinners?

A self-obsessed mind holding the mirror
to his cracked image of himself.

Hamlet's self-knowledge was all his own
It was not something that Ophelia could glean.

If thou wilt needs marry, marry a fool;
for wise men know well
what monsters you make of them.
To a nunnery, go…

How now, Prince, was that wisely
spoken to true Ophelia?

Orphaned, spurned by her Prince Charming,
she drowned, not knowing she was loved.

Ophelia died without any illusion.
It's the sort of thing lovers do.

THE SEAGULL

The story begins with a teacher,
Medvedenko, in love with Masha
who is in love with Konstantin
who is in love with Nina
who loves Trigorin, a minor
novelist in love with himself.

Trigorin is also loved by Arkadina,
an actress, the mother of Konstantin
who is in love with Nina-in-love-with-Trigorin.

In one inspired moment
Trigorin tells Nina a fable
about the shooting of a seagull,
about a man who meets an innocent girl
like Nina, near a lake in the country
and quite idly destroys her.

Nina does not listen carefully to his story
nor does she think before she leaps into his arms.
Nina wants to be an actress and Konstantin a writer.
Cocooned in their world of illusions,
both ruin themselves and each other.

He continues to love Nina and she continues to love Trigorin.
Trigorin continues to love everybody but mostly himself.

Nina calls herself the seagull that Konstantin
had shot, casually. Konstantin never deciphers
what she means. In one distracted moment
he kills himself just as he had shot the seagull.
And, thus mercifully ends a tale of unrequited love.

From *Numbering Our Days' Illusions*

LOVELAND

Next time I find myself in Loveland where things
are not what they seem, I'll be prepared with my mask
and magic spectacles, ready to join in the carnival.

When things go wrong as they do and will –
not in a predictable pattern, that would be easy to discern –
I will keep an open mind, let luck declare its hand.

Even a child knows love is not a game of abacus –
there is no advantage in matters of the heart
with experience, wisdom and all that crap.
Love selects its own company. Frankly, that's that.

Loveland is where you wander freely with no documents –
passports, visas, curriculum vitaes – nothing to declare
except your love in confidence, reverence, silence.

A palace of illusion, where everything appears familiar
but nothing is, in Loveland you never tango with reality.
Time passes, even that is difficult to decipher.

CITY SLICKERS

Helmeted musclemen gliding on steel escalators
in the City bomb-proof buildings against terrorists.

Space-walking on huge walls of glass,
they examine me as they would any other lass.

Smiling, they take a random walk unafraid of vertigo
like the stock market index raring to go.

Who said men seldom make passes at women with glasses?
Real men do, particularly at women in City offices.

Cubicles, now shatterproof, hold fragile egos.
Men in dark grey suits shuffle in corporate shoes.

Pin-stripe suits come and go, talking of P/E ratio,
top-down, bottom-up methods of the intelligent investor.

As I mend the rules of the old boys' network
and demand my share of the profits of my work,

I hit the invisible glass ceiling each time
I stand up for myself as if that was a crime.

A single, Indian female, I am trapped, alas,
in a cage of bomb-proof, shatter-proof glass.

The Jurassic laws in the City continue to spawn
dinosaurs that even Spielberg cannot improve upon.

Next time these helmeted musclemen blow me a kiss,
I will signal to them to rescue a woman in distress.

CITY LIFE

Getting up early, having gone to bed late
is City life, in between work there is no respite.

Markets keep the adrenalin flowing, giving life a buzz;
but these whizz kids are no match for the witches of Oz.

Analysts, brokers, consultants, directors of companies
advise me about investment themes and theories.

I organize company visits hoping to meet the ordinary
worker on the floor, though that is not deemed necessary.

Dressed in colourful suits, not the bland city grey,
I commute on the Misery Line for my karma every day.

Unskilled in the art of self-promotion, the rat race,
I fail to flatter the fragile, feckless egos of my bosses.

Watching myself drift sideways in organizations,
my mind moves laterally in new formations.

Excelling in my job as a stock picker,
I confound myself in my poor investment in a partner.

I have mastered the art of winner loses all
for not everything that goes down reverses its fall.

Nor do things I give boomerang back to me
in equal measure for then life could be *bon ami*.

I try not to become the weekend worrier.
I can't see the future through a rear-view mirror.

NAMES AS HOMES

What's in a name? You jokingly quote the bard.
Everything! Take mine, for instance –
Shanta Acharya, I introduce myself
and the faces suddenly go blank,
not the oriental sort that reveals nothing
but a Western impasse that conceals nothing.

I try to connect and negotiate
as I underplay my embarrassment.
Do you remember how *The Wasteland* ends? *Shantih*?
Shanta is the same word, meaning peace,
and Acharya refers to the enlightened one!
The exercise is only meant to break the ice,
makes a change from talking about the weather.

Most reckon it is an Indian sort of name
even though they can't pronounce it.
They enquire politely which part of India I'm from.
After all, it passes the time in a civil way.
I do have a pan-Indian sort of name and face,
quite difficult even for an Indian to guess.

When I say Orissa you hear Mauritius,
and recognition flickers across your face.
I feel guilty of having to deny you that much success.
Having lost our way all over again
we are on another journey through unfamiliar terrain.

I try a simpler route to explain:
It is south of Calcutta.
What's a few hundred miles between friends?
That usually works, thanks to Mother Teresa
and others who have laboured
to put Calcutta in the map of the world.

If I really want to expand your mind, I add:
If you draw a horizontal line from Bombay,
across India, it will pass through Bhubaneswar,
the capital of Orissa, in the middle of the east coast,
south of Bengal and north of Andhra Pradesh.
I grow into that dot in the atlas of the world.

From *Numbering Our Days' Illusions*

While it takes me two days to travel
from Bombay to Bhubaneswar by train,
we get somewhere over a drink in one evening.
My history and geography remain the same,
and I retain my name like an ancestral home.
So you see my friend there's a lot in a name.

TREES

Strange fetish of trees in the snow.
So many pagodas their arches seem,
consecrating the ground they half bury themselves in.

The fog meditates on ivory stupas,
revealing no passion only the landscape's anonymity.

Eyes under purdah see what lies are meant for,
knowing no adultery, no abortion, no self-obsession,
meeting the protocol of seasons effortlessly.
Charismatic ambassadors, leaves negotiate with the sun.

In this they are not trapped like Philomela,
their peplus offers no autobiography.

Freed of self-portraits, they do their vanishing mime
with the singleness of yoginis renouncing the act.

PYREXIA OF UNKNOWN ORIGIN

The sky is one blank silver-grey scroll
from my bed in the Princess Grace Hospital.
Perfect setting for a late-afternoon meditation
as I lie with a fever of unknown origin.

I imagine the maples in Westonbirt arboretum
gracefully conducting an autumnal sonata,
displaying with pride their magnificent foliage.
This season I have missed my annual pilgrimage.

The moon shines directly on my face as I
wake to an inky-blue negative film of a sky
with the globe of a fully exposed moon
developing in cumulous clouds' cocoon.

Piling blankets on myself, I measure the speed
of the moon, racing with the gypsy clouds in flight,
winking at me at the crossing of each Rubicon –
when the passage is rough the moon lies eclipsed.

Nurses and doctors come and go, taking my temperature,
blood pressure, samples of urine and blood for culture,
chest x-ray, abdominal scan, endoscopy, tests galore.
I lie exhausted, expecting the phone to ring.

I wait for you like a bare, forked tree in winter,
dreaming of spring, for buds and leaves to appear.
This need to live with you like an elixir
will cure my pyrexia of unknown origin.

From *Numbering Our Days' Illusions*

FREED OF FASCINATION

Last night the blizzard trapped us all.
Those who built the snowman in our square
renounced the sky to its antics after all these years.

Thirty-one winters, the weatherman last reported.
I was grateful spared of such annunciation,
trying to depart passionless through the door of the sun.

That pristine morning I woke up to the landscape
altered by an intimation of your coming.

You too had arrived unannounced,
ushering in ecstasy into my ivory singleness
with the candid breath of syllables:
Let's do it properly.

It snowed properly for days without end.
Our world surpassed all fulfilment of beauty.

After all these years not to be freed of fascination
meant that loving has mostly to do with being human.

The delicate flakes hardened to ice before the thaw.
Strangers who slipped on the slush cursed as they fell,
curses that had nothing to do with loving or giving.

I lived my days, equally vulnerable, unable to curse
knowing the sun will banish the snowman from my mandala.

FOR THE DISPOSSESSED

Each passion in my sinews' landscape
strives to encounter itself articulate.

Consciousness is captivity held in silence.

You recreated my womanhood
in the tradition of whoring goddesses

that tread this cultured sunshine
in a processional of marionettes.

Nor am I my self-conferred queen,
I cannot even define this becoming.

These syllables are familiar to me;
here is my space, but I cannot lie in it.

Then I must speak for the dispossessed,
the exploration is no longer the same.

WORDS AS PLACES

Images of retreating words mirage our unexplored
thoughts, travellers in an alien country –
unprotected self-portraits.

The images come straight through the masquerade
from the bottom of this immense pool of seeming.

This the defect of our too great nearness,
attributing to one experiences of the other.

From *Numbering Our Days' Illusions*

I can only have my personal awareness of you,
a ritual out of myself I must provide for.

You pinned all your metaphors on me,
ferocious alphabets scrawled upon my limbs.

Anywhere I grow I have to find a world elsewhere.

The landscape alters irrevocably with my coming.
I cannot have prior knowledge of it.

From Looking In, Looking Out

For Sanjay and *Binodini*
Sushanta and Madhumita
Bikash and always for Bapa and Ma

Each mortal thing does one thing and the same:
Deals out that being indoors each one dwells;
Selves – goes itself; *myself* it speaks and spells,
Crying *What I do is me: for that I came.*

–Gerard Manley Hopkins

Just Infinites of Nought –
As far as it could see –
So looked the face I looked upon –
So looked itself – on Me –

–Emily Dickinson

What is life but the angle of vision? A man is measured by the angle at which he looks at objects ... This is his fate and his employer. Knowing is the measure of man.

–Ralph Waldo Emerson

AT THE EDGE OF THE WORLD

(After Anish Kapoor's 'creations' at the Hayward Gallery, London, 1998)

The queue outside stretches
like an alley cat, waiting
to enter the crowded gallery,
explore the plugged-holes at the centre
of walls and ceilings. Not enough time
or space for all to experience ways of defining
It – of lending shape, colour, sound, meaning.

Once inside, the world is turned upside down,
inside out, disoriented with double mirrors,
emptied of space funnelling into arupa,
untitled, leaving us newly-born, fearful of oblivion.

In the beginning (or is it the end?)
securing a discrete position
I get sucked into my mother's womb
peering at deep dark shrines of
my body, her body; our bodies
moving in rhythm to creations
at the vortex, doubly inverted images,
when I become pregnant, making the world many.

We exchange according to our measure
the open-endedness of things, configuring
a nose, a breast, a man posing in his briefs?
Or something new waiting to be seen.

From *Looking In, Looking Out*

Imagination turns earth and stone into sky.
In the dark, polished hollow of a marble mummy
a fleeting spirit appears. A twisting column of light,
I flicker before giving up the ghost.

THE ANNUNCIATION

The book she held half-open, half-closed,
clasped between startled fingers,
her thumb, a page mark; the others curled
gently over the covers, slightly ajar.

Seized in a moment of contemplation, the spirit
of quiet ravishment had not quite effaced her.

The rich maroon and purple-blue sleeves of her dress,
embroidered with golden borders, caress the letters
of the illuminated script as the light of Gabriel
intercepted the direction of her thoughts.

The painting was a silent church
before the service begins. A time for waiting…

Did Mary have a premonition of portentous tidings,
was she prepared for the divine dispensation?

What were her thoughts when that voice was heard,
her trance shattered by the dove's laser beams?

What was the book she clasped in her hands,
her memoirs or a book of prayers?

What was Mary doing dressed like a queen
seated among the lilies and roses,
as if waiting for a rendezvous with a secret lover?

Did she feel the stirrings in her womb,
great white wings flapping?

MAKING FACES

(After George Grosz' *Fruhlingsanfang*)

Her fragile features float
above the voices –
rising, falling, swirling,
grand ballerinas of smoke,
pirouetting on cigars, pipes
balanced between fat lips
of aging men, moustached,
dark-suited and solid
on coffee tables encircling her.

The painting caricatures
all the characters in it,
depicting the times' depravity –
except this porcelain, unreal face
in *The Beginning of Spring*,
threatening to melt under closer
scrutiny, haunting the picture.

Her older, frisky escort knows well
the irresistible rising of sap in life's autumn,
a crescendo of notes in symphony –
a darkening sky illuminated with fireworks,
upwardly mobile sperms shooting
forth like champion sprinters, overcoming
odds, with a fascination for making faces,
creating a world of cartoon characters.

LOST IN AFRICA

(After *Africa: The Art of a Continent*, Royal Academy Of Arts, London, 1995)

Look, the hand axe from Olduvai
over a million and half years ago,
among the first things made by man,
no earlier artefact exists in museums.

Much later the arrival of the decorated
ostrich egg, needing no messenger
hot foot from the Nile to tell a bushman
that an egg is a readymade pot.

The five-thousand-year-old battlefield palette
(its two pieces brought together for the first time),
depicts a disfigured continent –
the scars, the wars, idyllic scenes of man and beast –
the Jekyll and Hyde union perfectly captured
in the Makonde helmet mask.

The showcase of the sensuous lips of Akhenaten,
the seductive torso of Nefertiti,
the haunting head of their daughter
reveal only the artist's attention to detail –
no directions here to the status of women.

Woodcarvings from the eastern coast
enriched by trade, smeared with toil
display the skill in carving objects
from a single piece of wood. Exquisite
the diadems of lions, crocodiles, snakes,
an ivory profile of a leopard's head –
dreaming of ancestral homes lost in Africa.

XOCHIPILLI

(After *Aztecs*, Royal Academy Of Arts, London, 2003)

Your journey from the island of herons
past the crooked mountains
to the place of the stone cactus
where an eagle perched on a prickly pear
and the first Templo Mayor was born
took centuries. Longer
to create a civilization carved in stone,
painted in blood, consecrated by gods
who sacrificed themselves to make
the sun, moon, mankind and maize.

To sustain the cycle of creation, Aztecs fed
their gods with human hearts and blood.
Divinity was all! Flower Prince –
God of poetry and plants, patron of song and dance,
you presided over public ceremonies,
staged battles with ritually dressed warriors,
capturing the enemy for sacrifice.
The priests clad in robes of gods were
transformed with juice of the cactus.

Posing for us at the Royal Academy of Arts
Xochipilli, do you feel at home –
seated upright, cross-legged on a decorated
seat, each side depicting a flower
with a butterfly sucking its nectar,
your limbs tattooed with flowers,
magnificent your mask with hollowed eyes,
chipped nose, lips parted in a wry smile;
your head-dress ornate with large ear spools
as much in vogue as your necklace
from the skin of the head of a jaguar?

THE MILKMAID

(After the painting by Johannes Vermeer)

Concentrating on the milk she pours
from one earthenware vessel to another,

the mustard yellow sleeves of her
rolled-up blouse reveal her sturdy arms,

the beige, purple and maroon
of her garment in flowing folds swoon –

highlighting her sumptuous, robust figure.
The light catches her in a moment of stillness,

her head bent slightly as if in prayer.
Brightness of freshly baked bread

spread invitingly on the table in front of her,
the kitchen utensils, a basket of wicker,

the foot-warmer resting on the floor
in one corner offer hints and guesses – nurture

with passion, a sensual aspect to her character.
Her attention is not lavished on the viewer.

YASHODA'S VISION

Krishna, barely past crawling on all fours,
full of a child's curiosity and love,
eager to devour the world
is one day accused of eating dirt.

His playmates complain to Yashoda,
Krishna's foster mother,
who, unable to ignore matters further,
is forced to chide her charge. She commands
Krishna to reveal the contents of his mouth.

As she kneels to peer inside this cavern,
she witnesses the birth of the universe –
the sun, moon, stars, galaxies,
oceans, earth, deserts, volcanoes,
animals and plants long extinct,
time, love, death, birth, pain, wisdom, joy –
not a life, leaf, stone, word, person missing.

Yashoda sees herself, all her past
incarnations, with all the dirt, the dust
of the universe in its place; for a moment
blessed with insight, the essence of Creation.

OF MAGIC AND MEN

In a Hindu world of fantasy and fable,
myths, legends, gods and demons,
irrationality appears reasonable.

The clear light of day obfuscates while chaos enlightens.

Liberals argue: If our gods can eat and sleep,
steal buttermilk, make love, fall ill,
go visit their aunt in full regalia,
brushing their teeth before partying,
what's so surprising about drinking some milk?
After all, it has been one long, hot, desiccating summer.

The believers devoutly rejoice: To us, a saviour is born!
As long as a search does not spawn a multitude of gods.

When a community unites in a willing suspension of disbelief,
experts agree it is acknowledging a deeper human need
to rise above the insignificance of our existence,
embrace the Beyond that represents our notions of God.
The world's a stage, remember? Question not the need.

Ganesha and Nandi, Lord Shiva's bull, suck milk
simultaneously in temples around the world.
TV cameras religiously broadcast these scenes
from a multitude of angles that prove or disprove nothing.

It is all in the mind, the guru-busters explain.
Their patience like the roots of a banyan tree
reaching out to educate the superstitious earth.

Magicians are no god-men, the making of ashes,
trinkets and rings do not amount to miracles.

Tough Seshan's degree in physics does not free him.
Sai Baba bends his mind with a navratna ring,
out goes his hard-headed, Harvard training.

Both sides remain united in the struggle.
God's in heaven and all's wrong with our world –

except miracles unfurl daily to the faithful
not impervious to the mystery of the universe.

From *Looking In, Looking Out*

THE FLY AND THE BEE

I am equally at ease
with the sacred or the profane.
I can sit indifferently
on sacramental offerings
or on things most foul to beings,
at home in both,
bearing the good with the evil,
hankering for neither.
I have that rare option.
The fly boasted to the bee
with some exaggeration.

I can only sit on blossoms
ready for pollination,
sucking the nectar of flowers
or in my honeycomb
dreaming of perfumed stalks.
Lamented the bee, acknowledging
its limitations with graceful candour.

SNOWDROPS

In the shadow of tall, sky-gazing trees
a convent of reclusive snowdrops
face the earth, bent in meditation.

Possessed in the white heat of passion
the gravity of their thoughts weigh them down,
their porcelain faces averted from our direction.

In translucent stems of jade and petals of pearl,
they arrive bearing the gift of life – nuns of peace,
breaking out of barren winter's embrace.

Messengers of hope, figurines of faith and charity,
fragile creations exuding dignity –
they give according to their measure,
demanding nothing in return, their miniature
stature lacking fragrance, not colour.

They bow, emptying themselves of all desire,
make peace with themselves without walking on fire.

AZALEAS IN SPRING

It was by no means evident
that the super-kinetic buzzing of bees
expressed any pleasure taken in exploring,
sucking the azaleas, full bloom in spring.

Nor did the bees behave badly, drunk with honey.
They appeared sober, gliding from bower to bower,
calm under the circumstances, robot-like,
displaying no emotion nor willpower,
going about their business, fertilizing each flower.

Nor was it clear that the fragrant azaleas
frigid under the dervish dance of the bees
felt any ecstasy during or after
the mindless marauding of bees.

The azaleas appeared to respond eagerly,
shuddering in passing gusts of wind.

THE ART OF EATING FRUITS

Dig a hole in the eye of the green coconut,
turn it upside down and drink all the milk it has to offer –
split it open, scrape the kernel, deep inside its belly,
then let the tender flesh slide down your gullet.

Hold the mango in the palm of your hands,
firmly seize the day with the gentleness of passion
as you close your eyes, squeezing and sucking a breast.
Sitting in the garden without knives, forks or spoons, knead
the yielding flesh, lick the sweetness oozing from the fruit.

Crack open the pomegranate like a brittle skull;
rubies lie hidden there, waiting to be crushed by diamonds
sparkling in your mouth. If you prefer anar juice, grind
the jewels into a vermilion paste as if preparing for Holi –
smear the colours on friends, turn them into modern paintings
instead of a canvas with finely chiselled, miniature portraits.

Pull back the skin of a banana with nonchalance,
bite off greedily its erectness. Have no patience,
it might oxidize into a limpid, rusty brown presence.

Pitted dates, prunes, figs and grapes are most pleasurable
when you crunch through their silken crepe fibres.
Play a game of spit-the-seed, suck-the-stone every time
you eat pears, plums, nectarines, guavas, apples, apricots –
they are best munched with the skin to imbibe their full flavour.

The art of eating jackfruit is acquired only by the artiste.
Protect hands with surgically oiled gloves of knowledge
before you prise it open, diving into its ambergris.

BATCHELORS SOUP

I arrived here, improvised, hesitant,
this is my life but I'm ignorant of the part.

I remain unaware of the script, unsure what the style is –
tragedy, comedy, miracle-play or puppetry?

It is poorly directed, difficult to decipher.
I make things up as I go along, being prompted
incorrectly to pull off stunts at the last minute.

I live in ignorance as I live in my skin,
there is none to question or clarify the meaning.
I do my best under the circumstances.

I have to act without thinking, be eternally ready,
not unlike the trees outside my window, looking as if they
could do anything – put their hidden feet down, like flamingos
and take off to distant lands, green messengers of hope.

Inheriting forgiveness, the gift of forgetting, I emulate living
instinctively like any beast, bird or creeping, crawling thing.
I came here programmed with my karmic DNA.

I try not to lose the day through sorrow or apprehension,
or find myself in contemplation of what is not to be.

I empty the contents of life's sachet into this fleeting present,
add passion to taste and a perfect cup of life is ready for me.

From *Looking In, Looking Out*

WHAT IS THERE TO KNOW?

A quarter of the world's people live in poverty
without access to food, shelter, health or education.
The natural resources of our world are finite.
In less than twenty years' time the world will
have changed in ways we cannot yet imagine.
What happens in the Middle East and Africa concerns us.
The need to develop trade will keep Europe united.
There will be little distinction between major political
parties, all over the world politicians will be marginalized.
The state will wither away and Marx will have the last laugh.
More and more people will work harder than ever,
and some people will never have any work experience.
More and more men and women will remain single,
have families with different lovers and friends.
People will live longer but die of strange illnesses.
Injustice will live as long as human beings do,
hope, love and truth have a way of surviving too.
Damaged people are not always dangerous.
Honey, garlic, ginger, turmeric are good for you,
charity, laughter, sleep and exercise are better;
they are not mutually exclusive, try them together.
Snakes are as noble as any other creature on earth,
will not bite unless provoked, and most are non-poisonous.
Most murderers know their victims.
Every day is a miracle despite what we do or don't.
Children give us a chance to change our world.
Each one of us is a very special person,
each one of us needs to discover this truth.

WHAT YOU DON'T KNOW

As a child you instinctively know
there are things you don't know,
you also know you know of things
the adults think you don't know.

Growing up is a process of knowing,
of knowing you don't know,
acknowledging that others might know,
though they don't know that you don't know.

Wisdom comes when you can forget what you know,
when you know your parents, friends, lovers, well-wishers,
even your enemies, your best teachers, don't know,
for what is worth knowing is what you don't know.

Some people are born plain lucky,
they sail through life without knowing
they don't know, and not knowing
they don't know what is worth knowing
protects them from a lifetime of unknowing.

For most of us there is a price to be paid,
most of us get damaged, more or less, in the process
and end up knowing what is not worth knowing.

From *Looking In, Looking Out*

SPECIAL

There is so much good in the worst of us,
And so much bad in the best of us,
That it hardly becomes any of us
To talk about the rest of us.

– *Anonymous*

There is nothing special about you or me
except our thinking that makes it so.
Some grow up thinking they are special,
others do so imagining they are not so.

It is our parents' caring or the lack of it
that makes us feel special or not quite so,
not the way we were made by our Maker.
That recognition comes in life much later.

Most nations believe they are special.
People who've lived together as neighbours
suddenly turn against each other and fight for years.
Others declare war for no special reason or purpose.

Most races think they are superior to others,
each has its Hitler and its Jews.
We are so special that in time we must all disappear.
In the interim, we pay the price for being special
not knowing if it was worth paying for.

There are times for feeling special,
times for remembering and doing things special,
knowing always it is our participation that makes it so.

There is nothing special about you or me,
there is much that is special about each one of us –
it is our thinking that makes it so.

EXPERIENCE AND INNOCENCE

Keep a thing by you
seven years
and it'll come in use
though it were the Devil,
said Experience
when Abaddon came recently into favour.

Unaware, I kept the Devil
seven years
locked in my heart
but learnt not its use,
wept Innocence
when Abaddon went lately out of favour.

PERHAPS

(for Nissim Ezckiel)

Perhaps we were never meant
to be like other creatures
more at home in their environment,
driven by instinct, their individual natures.

We pine for what we are not
and cannot be. Yet the moment
we are what we wanted to be, we want
to move on, our desires already spent.

Perhaps being unhappy, never feeling at home
is our only hope, our promised salvation.
Who can tell where this need will take us
as we pursue self-discovery to our satisfaction?

From *Looking In, Looking Out*

SURVIVAL

At the summer solstice the sun
in Cancer breeds vulnerable,
tenacious and excitable
crustaceans programmed
to triumph against odds –
in water, on land,
balancing their destiny
with grace, not unlike women
carrying water, firewood, children
on their heads, shoulders, arms –
the body transformed into
a miraculous vessel for survival.

Crabs, lobsters, beetles, scarabs,
snails, turtles, tortoises –
all self-contained, sensitive creatures –
supporting their crosses on their backs
negotiate in an uncertain,
unpredictable, unforgiving world,
making themselves at home everywhere,
being eternally prepared.

Alert to their surroundings,
shielding themselves from danger,
they adorn their armour –
faith that grows like leaves in spring.
For these guiltless warriors,
only one out of a hundred
of thousands will survive their spawning.

ICHTHYS

That we were here first has been universally recognized,
except by some monsters on terra firma who behave as if
they own this world. They make fun of us, call us names,
represent us riding bicycles or shove us up their smelly
nostrils, not the sort of places we normally like to visit.
Not that we lack a sense of humour, but enough is enough.

It was mainly the fault of that god-man who used us for his
miracles. Since then we have been a symbol of him.
Some species are backward in their understanding.
Why he could not settle for fruits or leaves is beyond us.
We like to help, we are more than generous,
feeding all manner of creatures with our flesh –
just prefer not to call it a miracle or holy communion.
Never imagined it would become a global phenomenon.

We would like to wipe out hunger in Africa, keep the world
healthy with our contribution to research in medicine.
We simply do not like wars to be fought in our waters
by those who have nothing in common with us. Our homes
are uninhabitable, we are left to survive anyway we can,
our gills stuck with oil, unable to breathe. Luckily, we know
how to multiply. Humans have yet to learn how to divide.

We do not like to be a commodity subject to demand and supply.
Even the most imaginative of humans refer to us as sex symbols.
We have entered a language that constricts our purpose and meaning,
appearing without copyright on seals, rings, urns and tombstones.

From *Looking In, Looking Out*

OUR FIRST MEETING

(for Ashish, Arup, Aditi and Isha)

My neighbour, who lives alone in the attic, comes
home at awkward hours and suddenly leaves,
disturbing me with his random walks as he goes
about his business when the world restores itself in peace.

It is difficult to say if he has a nine-to-five job,
it appears he's a bit of a loner and does not hobnob.
He scurries around clumsily like an underground rat in a hurry.
I used to think of him rudely as a fat pigeon worth a curry.

The walls of my ceiling are thin and my ears rather sharp.
I found his walkabouts unpredictable but settled not to carp.
Having resolved to ferret out his mysterious ways,
get to know the enemy, I said, sleeping soundly most days.

One wintry afternoon I heard him dancing on the rafters,
having swung in from the branches of the neighbouring trees.
Whether he was drunk, merry or suicidal was not easy to tell.
I was making some masala chai to pick me up, was feeling like hell.

With murder on my mind, the time appeared ripe for us to meet.
I opened the entrance to my attic, careful not
to frighten my rent-evading, tax-dodging tenant.
He was prepared too, not beating a retreat.

It was dark as twilight can be. I switched on the light
to see two shining ruby eyes staring back at me.
We stared and stared as it was love at first sight,
my big, brown, bushy squirrel of a neighbour and me.

The question mark on his tail unfurled in a farewell and greeting,
we turned away together, never to forget our first meeting.

LIVING WITHOUT CLEOPATRA

(for Jaysinh Birjépatil)

From her couch Cleopatra saw the bronze full moon
hanging like Captain Ahab's doubloon,
high on the mast of heaven,
reward for sighting the forsworn Other, the enemy within.

The moon was almost exactly at dead noon
in the sky-clock of the window when she woke in pain.
At the end of her memory there was dampness,
years of darkness as she struggled to remember.

The scene in the distance was an advent calendar –
windows lighted with goodwill messages.
The clock inside Cleopatra was ticking too fast
as she dreamed and sighed for her Antony.

He had been a sprightly puppy before disease and age
lathered him with fat. He breathed his last with his shiny
nose seeking her paws, their communication encompassing
the vastness of time and space. As age withered her
poor demented Cleopatra went barking mad,
baying at the moon as if she saw her Antony there.

One moonstruck night she sighted the forsworn enemy
and lunged at the double moon swimming in the pool.
Breathless, out of habit, she drowned, howling for Antony,
her whole world buried in the moving, waning moon.

PRESCRIPTION FOR GLASSES

The optician adorned me with asteroid spectacles,
removing my glasses, taking away my sight.

I was made to read the alphabets on his electric screen
first with one eye and then the other, but not with both,
letting it sink in that perfect vision was to be his gift.

We lingered in his heavily curtained, neon-lit underworld.
He sat in front of me, his scanning machine between us
as he concentrated on the state of my cornea, retina and iris.

The silence of the room was interrupted by his whispers,
urging me to look at the ceiling, floor, walls on either
side, follow his roving phallic finger with my eyes
as it hovered wildly within my arc of vision.

He bent patiently over each eye, studying their defects.
His fingers pressed on my hair and temples when he turned
my head to study my profile as if he was a phrenologist.

Do you see better in this lens or in this? he queried
as he switched lenses with the dexterity of a magician.
It was difficult to say: Is there optimal vision?

Much depends on how much you want to see,
he muttered, having explained my failure to see the world
as it is. His lenses had the gift of perfect sight –

he could mend long or short sightedness, astigmatism,
all aberrations of vision. Self-contained in a box,
unassuming, the powerful prisms of glass
stood evangelically between me and the world.
My life manageable with its ill-defined, frayed,
squinted edges. The lenses round fish eyes,

dependable eagle eyes, alert cat eyes, beautiful in
their glassy sheen, glittering clear as running streams.

Through the looking glass I could see every
thing pretty much anyway I pleased. The prescription was free.

DAILY REMEDIES

(for children of all ages)

Daily wash face with wonder,
brush teeth with honey and oil of clove.
Treat itchy eyes with dewdrops and rosewater.

Swab ears regularly with raga and symphony buds.
Massage body with sunshine and olive oil,
then allow to run wild in fields of grass.

Gently rub kisses into cuts and bruises,
let long hours of sleep cure aching limbs.

Treat tantrums with masterly indirection.
Listen with sympathy, slowly divert attention
towards anything that distracts from distraction.

Answer all questions with imagination,
feeding curiosity, stretching creativity
with stories taller than the mightiest oaks.

Deal with stubbornness in much the same fashion,
with games, myths, songs, magic and pure illusion.

OF POEMS

I

They seldom arrive at your door, ringing your bell
like the postman with a registered letter or parcel,
friends invited for dinner, Friends of the Earth,
or even the truant monsters from hell.

They are more inclined to trespass on your thoughts,
your dreams, appearing with their gifts
unannounced, unexpected –

flying in and out, colourful birds of passage,
demanding your undivided attention
regardless of your present situation,
whether you are falling asleep, at the theatre
or engaged in a business meeting.

They expect you to be eternally ready
for their reception – life itself a mere distraction.

Some arrive perfectly composed, babies
poised with perfect backbone and teeth,
demanding to be heard, seeking adoration.

Others need to be rescued urgently
with extensive surgery before they start breathing.

A few are lost irretrievably, staying on
in memory to haunt your lack of skill in delivery.

II

Poems are no different from children –
at first clinging to your inner being and soul,
inhabiting your body's every cell,
a permanent physical condition, oxygen in your blood,
defining your sanity, your personality,
any life you might claim to be your own.

Before you know they're born, they are rehearsing
eagerly to fly away, explore their place in the world.

Inexperienced and naïve, they are often misled,
the weakest ones the most susceptible,
trusting strangers with a honeyed tongue,
ready to strike up a dialogue, pretending to be grown-up.
Like many adults they end up lonely and misunderstood.

If one achieves any sort of distinction, the others
temporarily bask in the refracted glory of success.
If one is dishonoured, the rest are condemned to oblivion
though the family stands solidly behind,
providing undying support, proof of pedigree.

Years later, having seen the world, survived its slings,
embraced its wicked ways, returns the prodigal.

With a shock of recognition you observe a child honing home
with the curve of your lip, the bend in your eyebrow,
and you remember fondly the time of its making,
when word was made flesh, conceived and born.

TO BE A BEGINNER

If the angel deigns to come, it will be because you have convinced her, not by tears, but by your humble resolve to be always beginning; to be a beginner.

– Rainer Maria Rilke

The master artist triumphant,
celebrated by critics, feted by fans,
confessed to his favourite disciple
the secret of Art – the compulsion to create
endless versions of the One.

With each flawed creation, the idea of perfection
haunted his dreams even after an imperfect
world was revealed to him.

Days arrived wearing their diadem of gifts.
Carpe diem, carpe diem – he trilled,
a thrush from the highest branch in spring
never fully understanding its meaning.

He had yet to learn a few things, including
the art of removing the mote in his eye.

Never near enough to the Divine, he could not
see the connection between beings –

failing to experience the mysteries of the universe,
be enlightened with its promise of beginnings,
trusting the light would descend on him
the day angels sing.

THE SCRIPTWRITER

You demanded alterations every day,
you, whom I invented for a very special purpose.
I yielded to your preferences, noted the things you loved.

You wanted your separate exits and entrances,
yearned for a life that I would curse no one with.
I indulged your fantasies, imagining you would tire of it all,
sooner or later, leaving your world to me.

Your characters asked to be born and I let it be so.
The text had to be changed to suit your silly plans,
the plot went crazy and my stories floundered.

After all these mistakes, you'd think humility is possible –
as the scriptwriter I can force some sense into you?

I asked you to be yourself when I delivered you,
freeing you to overcome sadness and temptation.
How can I create when you restrict my meaning?

FICKLE FLAME

Swaying on tiptoe, a reluctant ballerina in discomfort,
past midnight, shivering in a bath towel in midwinter,
leaning against a draughty bare window for support,
I yearn for the all-embracing benison of a hot shower.

The shampoo in my unwashed hair begins to trickle
into my eyes. I fumble for the ignition button of my boiler. Heady
with discovery I press passionately for the flame to rekindle,
remembering to press repeatedly and hold until flame is steady –

as directed in the instruction manual now inscribed in my memory.
One finger glued to the redeeming button I am afraid of losing
the flame that goes out, again and again. Though weary,
I woo patiently, pressing incessantly, tired fingers aching.

I pirouette with joy when the boiler shudders back to life.
If only I had a button to restore belief, banish chaos and strife.

FLIGHT DISTANCE

(With acknowledgment to Yann Martel's *Life of Pi*)

Flamingos in the wild won't mind
our presence three hundred yards off.

Cross that boundary and they sense danger.
Get closer, and you trigger
a flight reaction from which they will
not cease until
that safe distance is re-established
or their lungs and hearts fail.

Giraffes will allow you to come within
thirty yards of them if you are
in a vehicle, but will retreat rapidly
if you come within a hundred
and fifty yards on foot.

Fiddler crabs scurry
if you are ten yards away.
Howler monkeys stir in their branches at twenty.
African buffaloes react at seventy-five.

Cats look, deer listen, bears smell.
Male seahorses flee, flashing a light of amber –

How far or near you am I allowed to venture?

TAKING STOCK

Why did he think adding meant increase?
To me it was dilution.
– *Philip Larkin*

I would not have bestowed my heart
if I thought you might break it in the taking.
Nor was friendship more measured in its giving.

There is no way of insuring our protection.
Whether affection lives or dies is a matter of grace,
which has to be earned in life like anything else.

Love need not be a puking, bawling, magical child.
There is no knowing how many ways
a mother can lose her flesh and blood.
The pain is always the same.
Life's hourglass keeps running.

Yet women enlist in this act of creation,
not addition nor dilution
just fulfilling nature's ordination,
lending our bodies –
sometimes there is no choice
in the manner of conception.

To have no partner, no child, no job, no security
is not natural to me. I cannot say this is exactly the way
I wanted it to be. Life has a way of turning out as it does.

We are not measured by how our lives evolve for us,
only the manner of our moulding it as it is briefly lent to us.

MY GOOD LUCK HOME

You presented me with two scarabs,
hieroglyphs etched on their lapis-lazuli backs,
from the gift-shop of the British Museum.
It's for good luck, you said.

I survey the pieces, their sacredness
treasured in the hollow of my palm,
imagine them alive, pushing the setting sun
along the sky, entreating my heart to be pure and light.

They nestle beside a coral stone and a pearl
framed in rings of beaten gold on my fingers,
charms given by my family to protect me from evil.

I find the Egyptian scarab couple their own home
away from the crowded open-house of my Indian gods,
transforming each corner of my living room
with gifts of fetishes from around the world.

Two Chinese cats guard my speculative angle of vision.
Even Ganesha travels with me in my handbag
to help me overcome obstacles in my adopted homeland.

The seven gods of luck from Japan smile on
as you eye my marble turtle god with its fine chiselled look,
its beady eyes, hand-crafted, appraising your secret nook –

leaving us with the legacy of an understanding –
the knowledge of what it means
to carry a whole household in oneself,
to be so perfectly self-contained, poised
at the centre of all manner of creatures unsheltered.

From *Looking In, Looking Out*

MRS KAFKA'S DILEMMA

While he was busy
with the nature of the universe,
the incomprehensibility of God
and other weighty matters,
she noticed a transformation in her.

When she sneezed
butterflies flew out of her nostrils.
She laughed and music emerged,
accompanied by a spectacular laser show.
Weeping had much the same effect
though the sounds and colours were sombre.

Her clipped nails she sold as rice-pearls,
her tears as precious moonstones.
All this amused her, made her popular.

The trouble began the day he metamorphosed
into a dreadful insect. The same day, wherever
her hairs fell, they turned into snakes.

Then a strange terror seized her –
she could finally get rid of him, perfect murder.
But could not imagine other men fancying her.
Annoyingly, part of her was in love with Franz.

She covered her head with a thick black lace,
plaited her long hair tight, refused to stir
out of her room, kept her door locked;
wore herself out hiding the wretched
creatures in her washing basket
each time they mysteriously appeared
(luckily they were harmless in her hands)
before despatching them to the forest
swearing her maid to eternal secrecy.

She dreaded her husband coming to see her
fearing that sooner or later
a single strand of her own hair
would betray her, making her a liar
for confessing her snake-hair killed her partner,
that she herself was quite innocent in the matter.

Perhaps her maid would vouch for her,
what if no one believed her?

If she could keep her counsel and pretend
she knew nothing about his disappearance,
could she then enlist the silence of others?

The uncertainty of it all simply destroyed her,
she knew not when these strange things
would stop happening to her.
She experienced loneliness as never before.

Nor could she predict the violence of her thoughts
if she were to witness a snake mating
with a gigantic insect before devouring it.

DEAR TECH SUPPORT

Last year I upgraded Boyfriend 5 to Husband 1
and noticed a distinct slowdown in the performance
of the flower, jewellery and other network applications
that had operated flawlessly in the Boyfriend system.

Husband 1 has uninstalled valuable programmes,
such as Romance 9, Night Out 7, Real Passion 10,
and automatically installed many undesirable programmes
such as Cricket 6, Football 8, and News Eternal 12.
The Conversation programme no longer runs as before
and House Cleaning simply crashes the system.

I've tried running the latest Nagging software,
adding a new welcome screen to our favourite settings,
examined all my folders, searched his documents
for evidence of infected files or commands
corrupting the Passion programme,
creative play centres and other functions.

Husband 1 has acquired a mind of its own.
It changes font colour when I paste kisses on it, whereas
the Boyfriend system had positively pinged with satisfaction.

The outlook for Messenger services has deteriorated,
access to weekly live-updates no longer excel
in their power and are never to the point.

I have viewed the automatic image utility function,
zooming in on dates and times of malfunctioning,
cross-referencing every word or programme
inserted, deleted, but cannot find any rhyme or reason.

What help can you provide, dear Tech Support, in restoring
Husband to the default configuration of Boyfriend?

DEAR CUSTOMER

Be realistic and not too critical, bear in mind
that Boyfriend 5 was an entertainment package
but Husband 1 is an operating system.
A whole new concept, they cannot be compared.

Try to enter the command C: I THOUGHT YOU LOVED ME
when you switch Husband 1 on next, then install Tears 9.
Husband 1 should automatically run the following applications:
Guilt 7, Flowers 6, Dinner-at-your-favourite-restaurant 8.
Remember, overuse of this application can cause Husband 1
to default to Grumpy Silence 2 or Happy Hour 4.

Note that Drinking Beer is a disruptive programme,
generating Snoring Loudly files. DO NOT install
Mother-in-Law or another Boyfriend programme.
These are not supported applications and will crash Husband 1.
No amount of rebooting or repair can then restore the system.

It could also trigger Husband 1 to default to programme Girlfriend 10 that runs dormant in the background. It has been known to introduce potentially serious viruses into the operating system. Husband 1 is a great programme though it comes with limited memory, and has been known to be rather slow in learning new applications.

You might consider buying additional software to enhance system performance. Personally, I recommend Hot Food 5, Single-Malt Scotch 7 supported by Black Satin Lingerie 9, which have been credited with improved hardware performance.

THE HOURGLASS

I lean out of your attic window,
a not-so-lithe gymnast in life's circus,
my legs balance on an unsteady ladder,
sometimes on your head and shoulder.

It was me who offered to count the missing tiles
on your roof, dealing with insurance claims
can make anyone feel lost. Floating in mid-air,
I am a pillar of strength as you mentally lean on me.
You suffer from vertigo, I have no fear of flying.

The Velux window seesaws, reflects your face in
the clouds. You stand on edge, streamlined as a stalagmite,
on the spiralling staircase, steadying me with your touch.

This can't be love? I ask myself as I perch on your roof,
surveying the texture of weather-beaten tiles with a field-glass.

I catch cats, birds, clouds, all independent creatures,
in my crystal cage instead of monkeys, peacocks, eagles,
and brightly coloured washing waving to the sun with
stranded paper kites stretched like bats on coconut trees.

I remember swinging in a garden on a rooftop in Bhubaneswar,
undulating with green fields and the concave blue sky –
divine hourglass, changing its features as I floated by.

Here we stand like soul-twins, houses semi-detached,
cemented in the middle by a wall of glass –
your hands connected to my feet as our glances cross over.
I climb down the ladder into the magnetic field of arms,
remove you further through the eyes of a binocular.

BROKEN GLASS

Last night in my dream you stood in the sunlight
streaming through my front door, your arms cradling
a bunch of bluebells gathered from your country home.
You had come to tell me about your wedding.

Your kingfisher blue eyes catching the light
as in a Vermeer, settling on me like the sea on shells.
You had taught me what it meant to be truly desired,
each pore of my body rejoicing in our insatiable carousal.

Our loving had been more brilliant than sunsets in autumn,
setting our two landscapes on fire. It took us days
to quench our exquisitely tender yet volcanic passion.
You wanted no other man to see the face of my satisfaction.

The bluebells were fresh in your translucent vase for days
reminding me it was early spring
        in the seasons of our knowing.

How did we come to such an unseasonal end?
Why appear now like an angel with your annunciation?

With each passing breath I died a little with you.
With each death I learnt to live a lifetime without you.

LOOKING IN, LOOKING OUT

You remove your shoes before you climb up the stairs,
a Velux window lies where the attic might have been.

A cupola of light makes all the difference to the inner
courtyard of my life. I am angle-poised, ready for vision.

It's an art gallery! You exclaim, taking in the miniature
prints and paintings, works of embroidery,
archways framing landscapes richer than tapestries –
pictures changing with hours and angles of light.

The old-fashioned windows in the rest of my home
rattle like an old nanny crooning me to sleep,
stirring me to open the curtains, let the moonlight in.

You talk about new programmes in word for windows,
lost in the realm of global markets and cyber space.

Is this how I'll recall your profile silhouetted
against the gleaming glass window,
talking about times to come, lives past –
as if talking to yourself, saying you've decided
to spend your birthday with your parents?

I draw the blinds, remember opening a shutter
in my ancestral home to admire the monsoon storm –
a lifetime of homesickness comes avalanching down.

Tonight we open another casement, switch on the TV –
watch helplessly how frail windows and doors can be,
failing to protect children and women traumatized
by war in their streets, bomb-shattered,
turned incomprehensibly into killing fields.

The news does not ease our vulnerability
as it moves on to places where hurricanes sweep
away homes, pillaging life and property.

I can no longer recall what it felt like to be truly desired,
I gaze into your eyes but can find no help there.

Only the memory of your voice:
            Wait for things to come to you.

As I wait for things to be revealed to me,
Life and Time have their way.

Love grows wings and flies out of hearts and homes.
Love, that many-splendored thing, will not stay
still, be entombed and expected to rise like a saviour.

If only we could save our feelings in files for windows.
I turn to the trees outside my open window.

The leaves have a session with me complaining
of their fate, of having no choice, no opportunity
to escape from the light of day, rugged chefs in green,
slaves of photosynthesis –

no freedom to fly the skies like birds surveying
the earth's artistry, eyes looking out, looking in…

The jharokhas of my mind are magical looking glasses –

desire dances feverishly on stained-glass windows of my cathedral,
swooning like flies against walls that limit my explorations.

From Shringara

In loving memory of my father –
Brundaban Acharya

And my grandparents –
Lakshmi and *Paramananda Acharya*
Swarnalata and *Ratnakar Sharangi*

Not, how did he die, but how did he live?
Not, what did he gain, but what did he give?
These are the units to measure the worth
Of a man as a man, regardless of birth.

–*Anonymous*

This is the hour of lead,
Remembered if outlived,
As freezing persons recollect the snow –
First chill, then stupor, then the letting go.

–*Emily Dickinson*

...It was love
brought him, as it brings
all of us in the end, face
against glass, to demand
brokenly of the anonymous: Who am I?

–*R.S. Thomas*

HIGHGATE CEMETERY

I wander among the dead in a cemetery town,
exploring winding paths where angels carved in stone
direct me through green alleyways.

This island with overhanging yew and trailing clematis,
unifying ivy nurturing insects, larvae, butterflies and birds
has more to do with the living than the departed.
We need solace of the Comfort Corner more than the dead.

Through the hawthorn and blackthorn, field maple and elm,
a cool wind blows steadily through our realm.

The voices of children from the playground
confirm the inscription on Karl Marx's tomb:

The philosophers have only interpreted the world
in various ways. The point however is to change it.

Every day our little world changes a little bit,
whether we like it or not is quite irrelevant.

I imagine a dialogue between Marx and Krishna.
It is easier I confess to alter myself than the world.

When our friends start to leave it is time
to take stock of our coming and going:

Of those immortal dead who live again
in minds made better by their presence.

In unmapped terrain within us we bury
in terraced catacombs painful memories.
If only we could let them grow out of us like trees.

LONELINESS

Sore red, splayed silently in pain, the dappled sky,
a woman bleeding, giving birth, dying,
sacrificing her body in a cycle of creation.

Loneliness is a mother holding her son crucified.

It is that lying awake at 4 a.m. feeling,
anaesthetized by faces of dead children –
Iphigenia, Irma, Alice, Shanti, Xian…
names and faces scrolling past from over the world.

Loneliness is coming home to an empty pram filled with toys.
Loneliness is when your young wife dies in childbirth.

Loneliness stalks everywhere, invisible like air.
Look in the core of deepest love, it is there.

Loneliness has been experienced at the height of ecstasy.
It is our saviour, learn to accept the gift of loneliness.

It is the human condition, a vocation,
passed on from generation to generation.

In it you can experience the road not taken,
the loneliness of a musical instrument untouched,
not breathed into, played nor caressed by human
hands. Loneliness is banished, temporarily,
when two people come together in love.

Loneliness is when you have no one to love.

Discover in loneliness the continents of yourself,
it's a secure place to wander in for nobody can trespass,
unless you let them in. It is an island of freedom and peace.

NOTHING'S A GIFT

Life's a gift they said as my treasures
began to be whittled away –
living a way of being repossessed,
our inventory infinitely detailed –
love, family, friends, freedom…

Living in debt, I've forgotten
when, where, why
I agreed to open a line of credit.
Was I hoping to be saved?

Nothing's a gift. Now I am here to pay
with my life, work, everything –
not a breath can I claim to be my own,
even this language my borrowed plumage.
We are here to offer an account of ourselves.

I learnt of ruined millionaires
promising to redeem our debt.
Uncertain, I prepare
the arrival of our Master of Ceremonies,
demanding my crown jewel –
not on any one's list, my soul, entrusted only to me,
my passport through time and space –
price of an invitation to this journey of a lifetime.

AJA

(In memory of my grandfather, Ratnakar Sharangi,
27 April 1907–2 March 2000)

I

The stars in midnight's sable shawl slip and fall,
tears from my eyes, snapped string of pearls.

Years back when I left the family cloisters –
each farewell a bereavement thereafter –
you urged me to be brave, fare forward.

You never wanted me to leave,
still you went with the flow, let me go.

Less than a month ago you blessed me,
your frail hand on my head –
affirming this meeting to be our last.

Watching each winter annex your freedom,
your passion for life ebbing like cinders
prepared me for your departure.

When I learnt you'd gone into a coma,
I prayed for a painless passage to pastures unknown.

Your spirit did not leave without a struggle,
body like slough of a snake cast off on an anthill.

In death you looked serenely regal –
your daughters recall times past, your life lovingly
wrapped in albums of gold and silver.

II

In Bhubaneswar the sun is rising
to greet devotees in the temple of Lingaraja,
keeping vigil for Shivaratri. Half-naked bodies,
disappearing in the morning mist of Bindusagar
rise from the lake, shoulder blades opening in prayer.

All through the day the cherry trees
in their full regalia recite their mantra: Carpe diem.
In time even cherished memories scatter.

I never had a premonition at the time of your departure.
They say when the soul prepares to leave
it severs all known channels of communication.

No point then in asking what thoughts
your mind was set upon as you were
summoned to step beyond our human limitation?
Did your guardian angel appear like an apparition?

If I try to tune myself to your medium,
can you beam your messages to me?

I will be ready, not fail to receive your signal,
misinterpret your purpose or meaning,
comforted by your appearances in my dreams
as memory holds a royal seat in this distracted globe.

III

You were blessed with faith, not struck with uncertainty
about the nature and existence of God.

I got lost somewhere along the way –
my faith changing colour like a chameleon.

I'd like to believe in a benign God.
Perhaps in my own sceptical way I do.

Doubting is one way of believing,
you reminded me to keep me in the fold.

As my notion of divinity keeps evolving,
I am content to leave the window of my belief
wide open, letting the universe in.

Our idea of Providence defines us,
trust time will make my image beyond wondrous.

If you possess a superior sense of perfection,
would it be possible to share It with us?

Let us know why God chooses
not to give better evidence of His existence,
nor intervene in our unjust world?

IV

You prepared for death with care
though we remained unappreciative
of the frailties of getting older, its strengths –
the body, most instructive,
as consciousness weaves in and out,
while memory moves tectonic plates,
playing with time, space and matter.

I imagine you a star in my galaxy
lighting my path, lifting my reach.

If you are able to pause for a moment
without affecting your progress
in the afterlife, I will be waiting for you.

The constraints of your body gone
you could visit me at home in Highgate –
something I could not achieve in your lifetime.

Perhaps you won't think of London,
this unreal city, unsuitable for your granddaughter?

Though by now you must know better,
places have their own karma and character –

Utkala is not what it was before,
nor Bhubaneswar the abode of the gods.
There may be halcyon places in the Himalayas,
but how can I survive there on my own?

I too am tainted, steeped in this metropolis
that sheltered my body, touched my soul.
Crocodile-like I am at home in this swamp,
unseen, unknown, watching the world pass by.

IN MEMORIAM

(In memory of my father, Brundaban Acharya,
9 November 1922–30 January 2001)

I

When you come to Bhubaneswar
          we will talk and talk for hours –

Words from your last letter
inscribed in my memory mock us father.

Luck, language of the universe,
mysterious chain connecting one with another.

Bhagya, destiny play their part.
          Impossible to tell them apart –
how much fate, how much character.

You never relished telephone conversations.
A few words of greeting and you were done,
handing over the receiver almost before we'd begun.

No longer can we communicate
now that you are gone. Number unknown.

What does it matter now what words I choose,
what order I arrange them in as they follow
            into a silence I know nothing about?

Unable to settle for words
my body reminds me it was never so deceived,
bursting into uncontrollable tears
without regard to time, place or decorum.

II

When I flew from your nest to find myself
you began to see the world through my eyes.

Now that you have gone, it is my turn to see
things the way they appeared to you –
the passage of time bringing us closer.

Twenty-five winters ago you suffered a stroke.
Wishing to protect me the family left me in the dark,
except I dreamt of your suffering and came home.

I've been visiting you like the seasons
year after year, celebrating our reunions.

The last time we were together
you told me about the devastating cyclone –
not a leaf far as the eye could see
            after the hurricane had gone.
It took a whole year to restore the family home.

Then Aja died within a month of my leaving.

We were coming to terms with his departure
when within a year of losing her father
our mother was widowed, a tree shorn
of leaves and blossom in an unseasonal storm.

III

Who can tell me why in the last winter
          you were to spend with us,
my annual pilgrimage to Bhubaneswar
was thwarted by my body's extreme exhaustion,
its struggle against viral infections?

My visit was never cancelled, just postponed –
unknown to me Destiny's course of action.

In January you had a cold.
How was I to know such a common affliction
would raise the risk of a heart attack fivefold?

When we spoke over the phone
          your voice gave no indication
of weakness or poor health. Even
          the night you were taken
to the hospital as a precaution,
we had not known the end was near –

no dreams, no premonitions, no hints nor guesses.
Had I forgotten to read the signs over the years?

          What use is evolution
if we lose the art of regeneration –
even primitive tadpoles have an edge over humans?

Who would want to be confined
          to Purgatory in a hospital's
Intensive Care Unit with strangers –
not the sort of sanctuary you'd wish for
when life is spinning towards a stasis?

Who can tell me why so vulnerable our exit
as our entrance, our privacy and dignity stripped?
Is that a necessary human condition?

IV

In the middle of the night
with none there to offer comfort,
you departed alone for another world.

You did not die, simply fell asleep –
boarding a flight in one country,
waking up in another
beyond our reach, our comprehension.

Was it better this way –
not to have said farewell, just fared forward?

Is death a country we are destined to arrive
alone, where even the chosen must suffer in transit?

We do not know what happened in the hospital,
during the hours you were there father.
Like so many blind men describing an elephant,
we struggle to put the pieces together –
the cause of your death unknown.

No doctor was there on call, fighting for your life,
none to hold your hand when the last breath stopped.

Perhaps we were spared our separate farewells
as we could never have endorsed such separation?

V

There is something elemental about cremations,
letting the body burn to ashes and bones.

Life reconfigured in space, time, conception –
the horizon a mirage of our limitation.

I was there father, my heart heavier
than your body when it was brought home
to be prepared for the funeral pyre –
your body a perfect likeness of its former self.

Could I have quickened you with my touch
unlike the petals, flowers, wreaths on your body
lying paralysed, unable to speak out in retribution –
          each cell in my body mutinous?

Could I have mixed my tears into the sandalwood
          paste stiffening on your cold brows,
pour my pain into lamps that burnt quietly
with incense rising straight up to the sun?

If I had followed you to the crematorium,
could I have summoned the strength to pray
for the liberation of your soul,
bliss and light perpetual beyond our shores –
without breaking down watching
Sanjay, your youngest, light your pyre,
the tongues of fire reducing you to bones and ashes?

VI

Grief is a lonely minstrel searching for answers
at life's itinerant fairs, looking in for a way out.

Like the soul grief never dies, only changes form –
a head shorn of its resplendent crown of hair,
an actor in fancy dress.

Death and birth adorn the journey of the soul.
Death the pilgrimage from where none returns.

If the purpose of life is to *Know Thyself*,
and the highest revelation is recognition
of the spiritual in All –
then grief too must enrich us
like love in the self-sufficiency of the Soul
which knowing no persons, no limitations,
no death nor birth, no divisions,
takes off its bodily garment
when it reaches home, the unmanifested Logos –
Love the only eternal thing in our universe...

LEARNING

When we look at one object
we turn away from others.

To keep awake in the face
of such elision is to establish
an original relation with the universe.

Learning not to turn away is prayer.

Let me not die to new ways
of seeing the world
born of this contrary time
in a multitude of lives.

Learning to reconcile difference is poetry.

To be blessed with vision is to be born again.
Learning to give without expectation is love.

Learning to love without limitation
is godlike, being eternally alive,
never having to turn away.

VIGIL

All through the dark, desolate night
memories of childhood kept me company,
with you steady as the flame
            keeping vigil over our family.

Grief-stricken, we lay stunned
explosions of pain shattering our epicentre
like the earthquake in Gujarat devouring families.

Silently we contemplate the unfolding of our lives,
its quiet purpose in bringing us together –
father, mother, brother, sister,
the relationships knitting us through the ages.

Where do our deepest thoughts come from?
Who brings us these tidings of love?
Are we like the earth yielding to the insatiable ocean,
being moulded into something new over centuries?

As we keep vigil through the night,
trusting the clay lamp to burn bright,
not flicker, leaving you in confusion –
        soaking its wick in ghee,
reading messages scratched on planets,
we hope all this will hasten
        the ascent of your soul
in its journey to worlds unknown.

I half-dream though half-awake
of you in exquisite colours,
rich hues of maroon, golden, purple,
memories quivering like fanned tails of peacocks.

FAREWELL GHAZAL

When I lie bereft, broken and dejected,
crossed by life, by the wide world rejected,

I rejoice you no longer have to face humiliation –
such is the fate of the human condition.

When darkness descends upon me thick as fog,
obliterating my view, turning my mind into bog,

I rejoice you no longer have to endure perdition –
such is the fate of the human condition.

When the slings and arrows of fortune pin me down,
leaving me to lick my wounds, blood trickling from my crown,

I rejoice you no longer have to wrestle with salvation –
such is the fate of the human condition.

When family and friends misunderstand me and each other,
grief makes children of us all, we cry and fight together,

I rejoice you no longer have to witness alienation –
such is the fate of the human condition.

When death can come in the stillness of the night,
take someone you love and you cannot put up a fight,

I rejoice you are no longer defined by our limitation –
such is the fate of the human condition.

SILENT WITNESS

Dad! … her words
slow thunder after lightning,
closing of doors, engines hissing,
movement of steel on steel, muffled
her litany of complaints in
the Underground station.

They pool their luggage on the platform,
he sits beside me on the empty wooden bench;
she leaves to find a map, her way to Angel.
I overhear her asking a fellow traveller.

It is difficult to tell whether he is hurt,
used to this sort of thing or simply a pain in the butt.
He sits quietly dignified, displaying no emotion.

When the Bank train finally arrives,
we get in together. He continues to sit next to me,
she continues to sit far away from him –
perfect strangers. Other commuters who join us
at Archway, Tufnell Park, Kentish Town, Camden Town
would never have guessed they were related,
thick as blood, father and daughter.

I want to tell her as we hurtle along
how time is short, not enough to squander
on pique, how sometimes there is not a chance
to hold a hand in love, touch feet in silent witness,
kiss a cheek, forehead, whisper farewell,
pray, do anything at all. Not out of choice,
but forced to face a lifetime without a father.

From *Shringara*

COCONUT MILK

My basket was heavy with shopping,
but the coconut milk was missing.
Sainsbury's did not have the ready-to-cook
variety, made in Thailand –
creamy as full-fat milk and just as silky.

Will this do? The shop assistant with a kind, withered
face handed me a solid cake of coconut milk.
I smiled, surprised. He smiled, shuffled off, satisfied.

That evening I cook the prawns
with finely chopped onions, mushrooms, tomatoes,
stirring in slivers of coconut milk.
The flavours waft through open windows into the sunset.

Moving to the rhythm of old Hindi film songs
you loved to hear, I savour your presence, father.
        The sun retires behind trees,
swaying to the raga and rasa of life –

teaching me that like the sun, moon and stars
you are always there, though briefly revealed.
When our paths diverge we must let go.

Sprinkling freshly chopped coriander leaves,
ground garlic and crushed chilli on the simmering curry,
my eyes are blinded with grief and a child's fury.

MISSING

It is that feeling on first awakening
to the matins of bird song,
your face playing hide-and-seek
as the sun peers through the morning mists.

My body moves into the light
as the day fills slowly with meaning.

I whisper your name like a mantra
as if the mere repeating of *Bapa*
can resurrect you. Even in my sleep
I know you are no longer here –
not just an absence in the family photograph.

A tree immersed in forgetfulness,
I am cursed to lose my leaves, dreaming
of buds, newly sprung – a festival of flowers
to rescue me from this bareness of being.

I dream of you and mother like clouds floating,
waiting all these years for my leafing.
I stand alone, your daughter, without offspring –
reaching for the foot of the rainbow.

Your features appear in every stranger's face,
lips transform into smiles in nondescript streets.

When the sun sets and stars begin their vespers,
I recognize the myriad ways of our losing and finding.

From *Shringara*

LOSING, FINDING

During a lifetime we lose and find legacies
dear as childhood, country, freedom –
even the realization of what family and love
mean may not come naturally to us.

By the time we are able to take stock of losses,
draw up an inventory of our inheritance,

Life plays its part, strips each asset
from the balance sheet of our heart,
releasing the riches of our past.

To know the true worth of our endowment
we must lose it first, unexpectedly.

Perhaps through some benign neglect
without any hope of recompense –
else time and knowledge make loss-adjusters
of us, we discount the past, present and future.

MORNING AFTER

(for those who lost loved ones to the cyclone in Orissa, October 1999)

Thinking we had seen it all –
floods, droughts, earthquakes, famines,
survived the deaths of thousands, year after year –
we prepared for this cyclone as any other.

How were we to know that heaven
would turn upon us,
not God's chosen, but godforsaken –
the wind would lock itself by night
into a narrow tract,
plucking out ancient trees like weeds?

Trees so old nobody knew their age –
the more stubborn snapped like twigs,
brave soldiers slain in battle.

The wind went howling, prowling
at speeds unknown to our ancestors,
more unpredictable than a mad elephant
on a marauding spree –
houses, livestock, the old and young
shaken like dice before being rolled out;
railway and power lines lay twisted,
giant pylons crushed like toys.

The rain got crazy too, hosing gallons
through barricaded doors, windows, flooding homes.
The wind like one possessed
battered incessantly, threatening
to crack open the fragile walls that protected us.

The ocean punished us without mercy,
waves marched in towering above us
twice as strong as the best of us –

living creatures were stunned into harmony,
shared their private space with the enemy.

Water crawled over the coastline like hungry crocodiles.

Morning after, the sun shone brilliantly
in a freshly painted sky with not a single leaf in sight.

LET ME GO

Let me go smiling, not blinded by light,
find myself on the other side.

Moving homes, continents, hearts,
taking what is needed, leaving all else behind,
slippers, well-wishers, memories,
dreams I cannot forget or remember –

dreams that keep changing
with time and place, maturing like a face,
a language, culture, the universe.

If only we could move with the grace of light
through glass, water, bodies, worlds…

like words settling for life not oblivion,
racing through the tunnel of time –
a child announcing its arrival.

9/11

I

We watched in disbelief and horror
when the planes crashed, the twin towers
of the World Trade Center collapsed –
moments that changed our world father,
reminding us of Nagasaki and Hiroshima.

How different this from the cyclone
that marooned Orissa when you were here,
witnessing the wrath of wind and water,
wiping out thousands of lives.
Is this the will of God? we cried together.

Bodies unrecognizable floated downstream,
sickening the stench of death – no barriers
to keep out snakes, scorpions, other poisonous
creatures, crawling in and out of flooded homes.
Families perched precariously on rooftops,
trees lay uprooted, branches accusing the sky.

Nor was this the earth's drunken dance
of destruction in Gujarat days before you died.
You took the knowledge with you
of what it means to lose your home –
lucky to be woken in the middle of the night,
a frightened spectator watching the drama unfold.

Houses mere stage props –
actors conscripted by a theatre company
to take part in a modern mystery play –
disappearing in a stroke behind the screen,
as the earth stretched and yawned,
a demon demanding unimaginable sacrifice,
except there was no return, no curtain call.

II

This was not the Great Calcutta Killing either
I'd witnessed through your eyes father,
before India was broken like a wafer
by a bankrupt trader turned master,
carelessly dividing a subcontinent
unceremoniously among Hindus and Muslims
who kept slaughtering each other.

There the enemies stood face-to-face,
eyes full of hatred, revenge, anger
as swords severed head, limbs and torso.

The victims of 9/11 felt fear
rise in their heart like a volcano,
caught as they were in a death trap –
no way out, no time to fight back,
offer peace, negotiate a deal,
come to terms with their fate,
say their prayers, their farewells –
as they were pulverized
with the imploding towers to dust.

All cremated in Ground Zero,
smouldering for days in one gigantic funeral pyre
of steel, pylons, wires, human parts –

Christians, Muslims, Jews, Hindus,
with the non-believers and agnostics –
three thousand lives extinguished in the holocaust.

Who can tell me what is worth dying for?
Are these the same things worth killing for?

REMEMBRANCE SUNDAY

When you go home Tell them of us and say,
For your Tomorrow, we gave our Today.

– An Epitaph in Kohima War Cemetery

They march by the Cenotaph
to the rousing bands,
stirring bugles of the Royal Marines
with poppy wreaths, medallions, memories –
each face a different story –
proudly representing their regiments.

These men and women fought for their country,
war-scarred, many died in foreign lands.
A host of possibilities bestowed on their lives
by war, a chance to die honourably –
the lottery of war making them heroes of sorts.

By the Guards Memorial they process like pilgrims,
twice born, blessed with life, hope –
commemorating the fallen with grace and glory.

This pomp and circumstance
is no more than an empty spectacle to the army
of unemployed youth watching enviously
the older generation parading across Whitehall
on other people's TV,
failing to win ten quid in the National Lottery.

LONDON: 7 July 2005

Flash of yellow light, blinding
the splinter of glass in my eye –
then silence as if thunder had lost its calling,
the brain's beating tide of blood drumming…

People wearing fear on their faces
like protective masks,
mouths distorted, screaming,
came pouring out of the tunnel –
stumbling over bodies lying
in the Underground station,
some unaware of limbs missing.

Is this our 9/11, terror unfolding?

Unable to protect myself from danger
(I had marched against the war)
I lay paralysed on the bloodied floor
each cell in my body a survivor.

Who would not rather live
with or without a god?

Trapped in hell, my thoughts were of you,
my children, you whom I hold dear.

Clinging to hope in a dark, cold corner,
fist wrapped tight round an angel's finger,
no longer a stranger, my saviour,
knight in shining armour, my valiant fire fighter.

11 July 2005

(On the tenth anniversary of the massacre in Srebrenica)

This cornfield once ripening with dreams
is now a monument to man's monstrosity –

a cemetery where bodies exhumed,
identified, are finally laid to rest.

Who can keep an inventory
of postcards from unknown graves,

from tormented souls wandering the earth
waiting for their haunted march to end?

Emptiness waits ceremoniously like tombs
as new places of genocide are unearthed –

a soccer field, a school, a hangar,
a quiet riverside, a bend in the road
where fresh skeletons emerge,
some broken, speaking of horrors untold
as chronicles of killings unfold.

Rough mounds of earth with green headstones,
names and dates of birth inscribed –
eight thousand victims, many teenage boys.

Graves untended, unadorned by memories,
none left to bring flowers. In this land
where every Muslim woman lost a husband,
father, brother or son, the bereaved left for foreign shores.

The flowerbed, the simple open pavilion
with a tiny crescent, a plain
slab of stone stands as a memorial
at Potocari with the invocation:

May revenge be turned into justice,
may mothers' tears be turned into prayers
that there be no more Srebrenicas.

WHAT MIGHT HAVE BEEN

(for Keki, in memory of Khurshid)

If you had not stepped into that car,
            the car had broken down,
the driver had taken a different route,
the traffic lights had changed. If only
someone had delayed your departure.

Any number of things could have prevented
your being at the wrong place at the wrong time.

If only your luck had not run out,
you had a narrow escape –
        an oversight, a diversion,
a horn, a brake, a nail, a thought, a cry,
an inch, an instant, a particle of dust in the eye –
as a result, because, although, despite...

A split second and the world changed.

BORI NOTESZ

(for Miklós Radnóti)

If I placed my faith in miracles,
        thinking there was an angel walking beside me,
do not judge me for my thoughts were only of you –
        I cannot die and cannot live without you.

I saw the blue of your eyes in the sky,
        shining like the angel's sword protecting me
as I fell, a ghost in the glow of dawn.
But I was lifted by invisible wings
        and marched on ignoring the ditch's embrace.

As long as I knew my way back to you,
        I was prepared to walk on live coals,
bear witness to the barbarism of human beings
        for man is the lowest of all animals –
setting houses, fields and factories on fire,
        streets overrun with people burning; men twisted,
springing up like snapped elastic, dead,
        twitching like broken twigs in the ditch.

Women screamed as children were dashed
        against walls: What is the purpose of this, Lord?
I asked. I survived, fixing my thoughts on you.
You were the constant in this churning, smoking mess.
I can only leave you my anger, my powerlessness
        at finding my world in ruins, left with neither
faith nor hope, compassion nor redemption.
        I know nothing can save me now.

If I placed my faith in miracles,
        thinking there was an angel walking beside me,
judge me only by my thoughts of you in a world rebuilt
        where my song will live and be heard...
I cannot die and cannot live without this thought.

LIFE? OR THEATRE?

(for Charlotte Salomon)

Take good care of it, it is my whole life...

With a few words you bequeathed
your legacy encrypted in gouaches,
double-sided pages of densely packed stories,
richly layered, *something wildly eccentric...*

Shot through with moments of intense happiness,
transforming the death wish in your veins
        into a celebration of life –
passionate, playful like the creations of Mozart.

In bed with mother discussing the afterlife,
you explored pain and redemption
raw with longing, urgent and reductive,
drawn from the colours of a childhood cradled
in a family touched with suicide, unravelling
after the devastation of *Kristallnacht* –
when *grandmother throws herself out of the window.*

Is extreme suffering the price of art?

For us there is hope and *Lezikaron* –
the looking forward, remembering the past.

Unrecorded your death –
gifted, young, pregnant;
perhaps murdered on arrival at Auschwitz?
Only an autobiography left with friends –
Life? or Theatre? A Play with Music.

THE FINAL ACT

(for Wisława Szymborska)

The most dramatic act is the one following the last –
the final curtain call, reappearance of the cast
on stage, raised from the wings
chorus and musicians, the company
adjusting wigs, make up, robes
as they line up to face the spectators.

The elaborate bows, ensemble and solo,
curtsey of the heroine and hero,
deep bow of the decapitated tyrant,
        the jester's farewell jig;
cheering of the crowd for Bottom
who could not play enough parts.

The encore of merry actors bowing together –
the victim smiling, holding the hand of his tormentor,
a nobleman rubbing shoulders with commoners.

The audience stirred, hearts beating
in the bodies of their enemies,
selves swept aside with the swish of velvet
screen, the readiness to re-enact...

SPEAK TO ME

The bunch of bluebells on your windowsill
is for constancy, there's honeysuckle
for devotion and affection. I invest meaning in flowers
as I wait for a sign from you in the retreating light.

I brought you field flowers to remind you of past times –
buttercups, cowslips, dandelions and wild violets.
Today I have come with potted jasmine for friendship.

Do you remember how we wove garlands for our pujas
with marigolds, hibiscus, bougainvillea, lilies –
flowers that were given by our neighbours to get rid of us
in the tree climbing, limb bruising days of our adolescence?

We took leaves of grass to decorate our handiwork,
left huge brass pots of palm trees to mark the mandap.

We painted the earth by night with rice paste,
you were best with Lakshmi's feet, I did the rest.

You told me magical tales under the orange blossom.
I believed in your words as we planted bashful
peonies, dainty daisies and virginal lupins –
watered the sunflowers that never tired of gazing at the sun.
Roses were incorruptible in your hands even as they blushed.

I could have worn a bleeding poppy. But I speak with its
shattered heart, knowing you cannot hear me. If I do your puja
with daffodils, lilies and iris, tendrils of blue clematis,
decorate your garland with deep green holly and ivy,
will you at least open your eyes and speak to me?

REMEMBERING GANDHI

Turning the other cheek you got the upper hand,
with Swadeshi and Satyagraha coined your brand.

Ace architect of freedom, the deconstruction of a nation
transformed you into a saint, to a shrewd politician.

You marched all over India to touch the Untouchables,
called them Harijans, children of God, and declared Home Rule.

Your fasts unto death plunged your peers into confusion,
transformed you into a saint, to a shrewd politician.

You trusted women, included them in your entourage,
your charisma, half-naked fakir, upset the Raj.

Your experiments with truth, sex and religion,
transformed you into a saint, to a shrewd politician.

The Viceregal Palace was haunted by your steel-rimmed spectacles,
your bald head, loin-cloth, wiry body, walking stick and chappals.

Man of vision, you rose above Nehru, Jinnah and Mountbatten,
transformed into a saint, to a shrewd politician.

What price we pay, in perpetuity, for the partition of our homeland,
the splintering of a subcontinent, giving birth to a wasteland?

Nobody understood you, Bapu, Mahatma of the nation,
transformed into a saint, to a shrewd politician.

In the end a Hindu fanatic reaching for your feet
lodges a bullet in your heart the moment your eyes meet.

Your life, a journey of self-discovery, overcoming illusion,
transformed you into a saint, to a shrewd politician.

ON FIRST READING THE *BHAGAVAD GITA*

(In memory of my grandfather, Paramananda Acharya,
29 August 1892–11 April 1971)

From an ancient land we came,
a continent vast as memory.

My grandmothers went there
first, raising families, dying in childbirth –
their rivers untamed, breaking boundaries,
appearing in me, my lost jewels, my shringara.

You too left to explore this place of reckoning.

Encouraging me to read, you never reprimanded
me for borrowing books from your library,
forgetting my chores reading under a tree.

Books opening like wings,
offering me in its fold worlds within worlds,
lifting my desire to discover life's meaning.

You gifted me the Song of God, the *Bhagavad Gita*,
blessing me with insight –
urging me to explore the universe,
find the temple buried deep in us,
see things as if for the first time.

Until grown old with knowing, loving,
losing, finding I can anchor at your island,
rich with all you have given me.

From *Shringara*

REMEMBERING

After great pain, a formal feeling comes.

– *Emily Dickinson*

The more I try to forget the more I remember.

From now on I will accept ceremoniously
whatever thoughts come unbidden to me even in my sleep,
feelings that burst through the mists of my nervous forgetting,
memories of you that moisten my startled eyes as life's gifts.

When I listen to your CDs of Mozart, I will let the music
fill the infinite between our two souls, not try to measure
the extent of my loss. What good is there
in speculating about what-might-have-been?

I will not build a Pyramid or a Taj Mahal to our friendship,
nor will I let the echoes of your words trapped in my limbs
haunt me like ghosts entombed in more formal relationships.
I will let the winds of change scatter my pain like ashes.

I will not change the locks to my heart, body or soul,
nor will I wait for your letter or phone call.

I will be patient like a stone and let Time be my counsellor.
Perhaps the less I try to forget the less I will remember.

THIS CONNECTION

Clusters of pods from branches of hornbeam
hang like Chinese lanterns pregnant with dream –

tales of transformation witnessed collectively
is theatre, experienced solo becomes prayer,
the journey from chrysalis to butterfly,
waking with desire, an aviator defying gravity,

a mountaineer scaling peaks drawn
out from the core of a changing world,
spinning, tiptoeing on a slippery slope

like trust in the face of uncertainties,
luck when the chapter of life is coming to a close,
alchemy turning the worst in us to our best,

unafraid of failure, taking risks, following our dreams,
seeing for the first time, eyes and mouth

opening wide with wonder, lovers swirling
in ecstasy on the dance floor, walking

on top of the world, bottom of the sea together
like earth moulded by wind, water, ice and fire,

knowing time will change all we cherish in our globe
taut as a belly with foetus becoming human

where we like gods are defined by what we are not
except Love that is everything and excludes nought.

SLEEP

Sleep comes to my troubled terrain
like the god of rain to parched earth.

Drinking freely at the fountain of forgetfulness –
even my days a kind of sleeping, not remembering –
        I am a bubble on a stream.

The landscape of my inner being replenished,
I yawn and stretch the taut skin of my sky –
Shiva's drum – ready for the dance to begin.

It is terrible to live with memory,
the beginning of all our suffering –
nor is it possible to navigate the treacherous
islands of Time without memory.

Life urges us daily to move on,
        follow the seasons, keep faith,
not sink in the sucking bog of our shifting past.

I learn to alter my mental habitat,
transformed into a creature that knows
its way instinctively through life's quicksand
        to sleep's precious cavern,
safe as chrysalis dreaming in its cocoon.

Miracle worker, lover, trusted friend –
sleep arrives with seven gifts of the spirit.

Giver of life, rescuing me from oblivion,
sleep opens my eyes, reveals to me my metier.

DREAMS

Stepping out of my skin –
my sack of bones, blood, muscles, organs,
an intricate network of connections,
imperfections, anxieties, hopes, loves,
of having been let down, having let others down –

I float free in a galaxy of myths and science fiction,
with no help from drugs or drinks,
remember nothing at all, no detail of events,
          people, places or things.

          I slip back into myself,
rested like the sky at dawn, daring to carry on –
a jukebox playing the same tunes again.

It's a feeling that lingers briefly on waking,
starlight banished in the morning,
overtaken by a sense of purpose,
          of nearing one's destination –
a sense of satisfaction as the train chugs into the station.

Closing the book I am reading –
          the story incomplete,
I continue with my journey,
knowing nothing else mattered.

WINTERING

All through the summer you stood there like a carnival-float,
displaying your pageantry of leaves, brightly coloured fruits.

You fed the birds, kept the children entertained – the wind in
your leaves singing stories as they played in our garden.
Irrepressible the excitement of horse-chestnuts in bloom.

In the silver light of the moon you woke me with your rustling,
your leaves shimmering as I lay listless in bed, the philandering
wind caressing while I slept with my window wide open.

In autumn you turned the knife deep in my heart with your
flaming colours. I saw no remorse in your celebration –
no damaged tissues or broken branches, no sign of exhaustion
as you flirted with the hours endlessly, ignoring my solitude.

Why stretch your bare arms in winter's deep embrace,
strong and swarthy, raised towards the sky like a spoilt child
crying, a devotee engaged in some eclectic worship?

What use is grief or prayers for your loss of leaves and flowers?
What grace do you imagine in the ebb and flow of sap, in your
gnarled, forked branches dreaming of forests of sequoia?

ALMOST

(In memory of Ken Smith)

You can be the richest person on earth and be happy, almost.
You can win the lottery and become a millionaire overnight.
You can be famous, list your bonds on the stock market.
Or go bankrupt, die of shame and regret, almost.
You can live happily in good health, in peace with your
Neighbours, almost; or you can fight each other forever.
You can be almost anything you want to be in your dreams –
The Milky Way, Beethoven, Shakespeare or Michelangelo.
You can fly to the moon, or just be yourself, happy, unknown.
Some days you feel on top of the world walking the streets.
Some days you fear losing almost everything in an instant,
Be swept off your feet by UFOs or killed in an accident…
Unlimited possibilities are not given to human beings,
If they were our lives would dissolve in the boundless.

HERE, NOW

Life is here, now
          seized in a moment's joy,
like zikr, remembering all is divine,
the truth for which we pine.

No words to describe
what remains in us of our samskara –
traces of our ancestors, our shringara –
this world, our ornament
          making us who we are.

Yet nothing, everything touches –
the fountainhead gushing from within us,
moving like a lover,
          graceful as lightning,
creating us new with each drop of time.

Making us not fearful, not holding back,
          not simply doing one's duty
but fulfilling ourselves,
taking flight like the smile of a camel.

SHUNYA

It took centuries
the journey from cipher,
invisible wedge, a thing of no importance
to zero, point of reckoning –
piece of the unknown fathomed,
being counted, standing solidly
three dimensional, banishing mystery
altering lives forever,
establishing one's significance
in space, time, trade, science,
lending the world order,
measuring phenomena,
not just the freezing point of water,
creating certainty,
holding things together.

Shunya, vessel taking the shape
of whatever is poured into it,
godlike, containing everything and nothing –
pregnant with possibility,
poised between positive, negative,
life and death,
vanishing point, knowing infinity,
drawing down divinity,
reflecting sum of the universe,
reducing all to Itself, always transforming...

I DO NOT KNOW

(After Shaikh Fakhruddin Ebrahim Hammedani)

Are you the universe and all existence,
in all things and beyond all things?
I do not know...

Are you the breath that keeps me alive
or the moments that take my breath away?
I do not know...

Are you the slayer or the slain, both or neither,
I do not know...

Why does your omnipotence tolerate
so much injustice in this world?
I do not know...

Are you immanent or transcendent,
unknowable or the One reaching out to us?
I do not know...

Do you pour suffering on us
    to mould us towards your purpose?
I do not know...

When I find doubt reigning supreme in my heart,
    is that also your way?
I do not know...

Why do you hide from your creation?
I do not know...

I thought I had an understanding with you
    but you took it away years ago.

Did you replace it with a superior covenant
    or simply renege on our contract?
I do not know...

If I cannot find you in my heart,
    in living creatures, in the eyes of my enemies;
where can I go looking for you,
    let me know for I am tired and bewildered.
I do not know...

If I cannot see your beauty, recognize
    your magnificence, what hope is there for me?

You taught me to find nothing in my heart
    except the compassion of your Love
And yet I do not know...

When will I be released from this separation;
    where do I end, and you begin?
I do not know...

THE LAST ILLUSION

Lying awake like the sky all night
I fall asleep with the promise of dawn,
waking in a land of rainbows
beyond our universe,
part Vegas, part Himalayas,
welcomed by an unfamiliar God.

Not the gods, goddesses, saints, saviours
I had grown accustomed to –
no parents, grandparents, ancestors, friends.
All believers of truth, goodness, integrity
and other such virtues were despatched to earth
to pay their dues, mend lives blighted by ethics.

The gods to themselves kept Justice,
humans held on to Hope –
the strong, pure in mind and action
believing most in divine retribution.

Ushered into this transcendent realm
I encounter history's countless evil men.
These were no monsters regaling me
with stories of their inhumanity.

Smiling at my shock of recognition,
the last illusion,
their bacchanal proceeded without interruption.
I was summoned to join in their celebration.

What any human knows is finite,
what we do not know is infinite...

Angels singing carry me back gently to myself
leaving me to figure It out.
I am woken by the cold, clear light of day.

SHRINGARA

The image in the mirror is no longer frozen
in an unimaginable longing.

A participant in life's carnival, I prepare for illusion.

Elizabeth Arden's flawless finish foundation frosts
on skin breathing Shahnaz Hussain's sandalwood face cream.
Givenchy's mascara thickens and lengthens eyelashes,
rosewood powder blushes on cheeks. My mask is complete
with desire red, double colour, everlasting Estee Lauder lipstick.
I spray myself generously with Nirvana and Samsara.

I travel towards what end I cannot say –

Along the way, those I meet and those I do not,
all the things that happen to me and those that do not
keep defining me in some inexplicable way.
Daily the mirror mocks my wrinkles, streaks of grey.

If I am the result of unrepeatable circumstances,
what use is there in seeking escape from self-enunciation?
In the end we are all dead. The days become my shringara.

From Dreams That Spell the Light

For Anisha, Anshuman, Abhirup, Aditi and Amrisha

The real voyage of discovery consists not in seeing new landscapes, but in having new eyes.

–*Marcel Proust*

We shall not cease from exploration
And the end of all our exploring
Will be to arrive where we started
And know the place for the first time.

–*T.S. Eliot*

ITALIAN PRAYER

How does one accustomed to the cold candour of stones
bend one's knee in reverence to the opulence of marble?

How does one sustain the journey from Konarka to St Peter's,
from Lingaraja to Santa Maria del Fiore, from the temple
of Jagannatha to the basilica of San Marco?

It is easier to let the mind auto-focus when set in poverty,
pain and austerity, to catch a glimpse of divinity,
crying out for help, the public prayer of the devotee,
without any signs saying '*Silence*' or '*For Private Prayers Only*'.

Teach me how to find myself in these palaces of art,
that I may learn to love and suffer with all my heart.

Teach me how not to be distracted by these treasures,
the tapestry of mosaics, paintings and sculptures,
by Michelangelo, Botticelli, Raphael,
Tintoretto, Leonardo da Vinci, Caravaggio.

Teach me how to empty my desires in this *Chiesa d'Oro*,
pray in a corner ungilded with the wealth of this world.

Teach me to light a steady candle in the sanctum of this cathedral,
rein in my wayward senses and learn to pray in this temple.

MOSQUE OF WAZIR KHAN

Rambling through the bazaars of Lahore,
cramped in the middle of the marketplace, I discover
Wazir Khan's mosque, its bejewelled decor.

Once a celebration of magnificence,
a thriving enterprise between commerce and learning,
the mosque has now lost its calling.

Decorated tiles, once emblazoned on every surface,
now haunt the edifice's aging, uncared for façades.

I remove my chappals, cover my head out of respect,
as I step through the gateway into the forecourt.

Moving from one world into the next,
I enter paradise on earth, I am blessed.

My guide translates one inscription for me –

Whatever is sown by man in one life is reaped in the next,
in your dealings then, be pure of heart.

KABUL: 14 November 2001

Standing in front of the mirror
combing back his hair, he encounters
a long-lost friend, a stranger,
never having seen his face without a beard
except when too young to remember.

His face looks gaunt though finely chiselled
in rock, the skin smooth and shining,
melting ice. He has tasted honey in freedom,
having discarded his facial mask.

It took the barber in the market an hour
to retrieve his face from beneath the rubble
of beard, five years of forbidden fruit.

His wife hums in the kitchen, immersed
in the ceremony of making tea –
singing to tunes playing on the radio
which has also emerged from purdah.

Her long raven hair declares liberty,
resplendent testimony in the setting sun,
her face smiling after an eternity –
she is expecting their first baby.

His gaze is glued to her face in the mirror.

She has never known peace in her time,
nor could he remember what it was like
when men grew old and the land was green.

In the distance bombs keep shattering
the silence of the surrounding ruins.

MIDNIGHT STROLL

(In the Sabo Quarter of Ibadan, for Jon H. Stallworthy with acknowledgement to 'Singing School')

A sea of tiny wick lanterns
keeps the kingdom of darkness at bay.

Behind each lantern scarred faces
fall constantly through light to shadow.

In the bazaar squat sellers
of bread and dried fish, silks and slippers,
kola nuts and cassava, tinned food and palm wine.

Here the maimed cast aside their crutches,
the paralysed beggar forgets his pitch
under the flame tree in the glory of dancing
to the frenzied drumming, shaking, bowing
of the magic music-makers.

The blind regain their sight
on round grass mats, deal out greasy cards,
flicked into a central pile,
pulling in precious pennies and sixpences
with great claw-like fingers.

POSTCARD FROM ST. PETERSBURG

We shall meet again, in Petersburg
– *Osip Mandelstam*

No map could have illustrated its character,
the past century's schizophrenic survivor.

Negotiating our way through the crowds,
we arrive in Palace Square,
unprepared for the treasures of the Hermitage.

A mirror of façades, the majestic Neva
barricading the revolution each day in our heart.

We greet the Bronze Horseman crushing treason,
haunted by the fate of Pushkin.
As we leave Yusupov's Palace,
a prayer escapes my lips for Rasputin –
Russia crushed with the weight of its past.

How different from Dostoevsky's dark world
the light in Sennaya Ploshchad; its tree-lined
canals, a haven for all during White Nights,
perfect after *Swan Lake* at the Mariinskiy.

Strolling down Nevsky Prospect, buying caviar
at Yeliseev's, window-shopping at Gostiny Dvor
and Passazh Arcade, its glass canopy turning
sky into ceiling, letting the sunshine stream in.

We emerge at the colonnades of the Kazan Cathedral,
taking in the view across the canal with a church
gleaming in the background, beckoning us
to pray for paradise built on bones and spilled blood.

BRYCE CANYON

(for Bikash Acharya)

We haven't got all day, you muttered,
vanishing into the mist,
ghostlike, though you stood a few feet away,
waiting for the fog to lift,
our day's sightseeing to begin.

Travelling through Time's creations,
nothing mattered, not even the here and now.

The universe was wrapped in a shawl of mystery
that gave no hint of shrugging itself off.

We waited, anticipating what lay beneath it all.
Beneath each human garment the soul,
beneath the mist testimony of stones.

For an instant, the playful mist shifted a little,
revealing a naked shoulder of exquisitely carved laterite,
the grandeur of a classical symphony in rock.

Obliterating us again from each other's vision,
the mist played upon us –

one moment appearing solid, unshakable,
the next dissolving in the tenuous
bond between brother and sister.

More sophisticated than any of our childhood
games, experimenting with make-believe,
wanting to make each other vanish,
            then reappear magically –
each time failing with one or the other,
unpacking the gift of miracles in our daily lives.

THE GREAT WALL OF CHINA

Gasps of wonder, flash of cameras, the bling-bling
of tourists, sound that light makes reflecting

off chrome, platinum, diamond or silver –
not the silence of stones, earth, blood and tears.

Forgotten the story of each farmer in the making
of a fortress, facing up to one's enemies, climbing

steps like a soldier. Each tower inscribed
with the names of families, villages that sacrificed

sons, the strong serving best the season, its purpose.
The weak and diseased immured in these
fortified walls, some considered it auspicious.

The voices of missing children trapped in posters
echo among the surrounding orchards of apricot trees.

Women hold vigil for their stolen offspring,
faces lit by lanterns flicker in the breeze.
Every child gives birth to a mother.

Silent stares transmit stories to strangers,
secrets survive under the skin like viruses.

Empty arms, haunted with memories
of sleepless nights, hear the silent screams

of skeletons in unidentified graves waiting
to be laid to rest, daughters disappearing like dreams.

Time sits on its haunches, Laughing Buddha,
indifferent the lofty ranges of soul mountains.

THE SUNDARBANS

I

A strange, wild place fed by the Ganga,
sweeping across the plains of Bengal
to the Indian Ocean. Here are no boundaries

keeping fresh water from salt, river from sea,
land from water, island from island.

The pure of heart venture into its labyrinth.
Only the true believer can fathom
its secret waterways, decipher its currents.

Their travel through awkward lands
are brief ruminations written on their hands.

Men dispossessed foray into its forests
for food, fish, honey, fresh berries,
wood, even tiger-parts, rich relics.

The strong and fearless enter this
immense archipelago of islands –
some treacherous, vast as cities,
others shifting sandbars of dreams.

II

The settlers set sail in boats on the back
of hungry tides, their only protection
the blessing of sea-faring gods and ancestors.
Women pray as their men take to the oars.

Lives, flickering like earthen lamps,
nestle in tiny bowls of flowers, leaf-wrapped,
sail along banks of the swollen Ganges.

All migrations leave scars.
World on the move, moving worlds –

Sun flashes tinsel on waters blessing the festivities.
They race ahead unafraid of their destiny,
holding their nerves steady in the face of enemies –
man-eating tigers, crocodiles or killer bees.

The men signal to each other like river dolphins
navigating their way through massive
aerial roots of ancient mangrove trees,
diving deep into dark dreams of waters.

III

Honey trees hum heaving with hives –
ten metres is the closest a man may come
near these champion bees without reprisal.

Fierce warriors, they flee on smelling smoke,
sensing danger – as elephants retreat
on hearing the approach of killer bees –
surrendering their hives heavy with liquid gold.

Tigers having traced a near-perfect habitat –
salty water makes them aggressive,
sacrifice fresh water among these shifting islands –
roam free in their new found land.

A twelve-year-old tigress, one canine missing,
patrols the village with a gap-toothed grin.

Tonight she is sated, has no desire to hunt or kill,
just observes from her retreat the children
in the mangrove trees swaying like jackfruit.

Clouds mass on the horizon –
the darkening sky pierced by snakes of lightning
turn the pages of a celestial symphony.
Thunder rehearses its beats in megh malhar.

IV

As the rains arrive, rice paddies replace wetlands,
giant apple snails and bull frogs clear the fields
of insects and algae, each field an entire ecosystem.

Open-billed storks hunt in rice fields,
welcomed by villagers as an omen of good luck.

Birds colonize the tops of trees,
breeding in the heart of bustling shanties,
black and white wings hover like clouds.

Fishermen follow the fabulous otters flushing
out shoals of fish. Not for the faint-hearted
such pleasures, hunting best when hungry.

As the tides recede myriad creatures,
strange and beautiful, emerge from their burrows
in this constantly changing scene –

mud skippers, fish and reptile in one,
fins transformed into legs for wading on mud.

Fiddler crabs sift food from the rich alluvial silt.
Alpha male crabs with huge claws ward
off rivals. Starlings feast on insects
after the rich harvesting of rice crops.

V

After the monsoons, rice fields turn from green
to brown. River banks come alive with the conversation
of mynahs. Butterflies dance with dragonflies
while dogs chase squirrels without a care in the world.

The river runs slowly like an aging grandparent,
boats are pulled against the tide by boys. The land
is parched, women dig for sand in the river bed.

It is the season for renovating homes.
Women paint themselves after decorating
the mud walls of their huts, balancing a paste of rice,
turmeric and vermillion on their fingertips.

The womb of the Ganga lies dry and empty,
a dust bowl of ashes, parched under the fiery sun
intense with expectation of the first shower –
blessed and blessing the first rain.

As the riverbed warms up like an oven,
villagers move in, spreading out to dry
their catch of fish, fishing nets, boats.

The stench sends a signal to wild boars
that sneak in to snack on desiccated fish.

The tigress roams impervious
to the stinking fish and spotted deer,
kingfishers and herons, crocodiles and cobras.

Ganga, the river goddess, may yet lose her power,
failing to reach the delta of her dreams.

The Sundarbans may one day disappear,
leaving no man fit to take the measure of another.

ASPECTS OF WESTONBIRT ARBORETUM

If you can discover the first leaves of honeysuckle unfolding,
fly fearless on a magic carpet of snowdrops in spring.

If you can rejoice with the flowering cherries in April,
tall columns of mahogany-red bark crowned by clouds
of blush white blossom, fragrant brides against the sky.

If you can be startled by clumps of primroses in bloom,
by bluebells waist-high, a purple haze on the woodland's floor,
by orchids, wild garlic and dandelions, you will encounter
the spirit of the arboretum exuding from each leaf and bower.

If you can watch the bumble bee tumble out of a foxglove's throat
and hear the laughter of Silkwood ringing through The Link.

If you can rest in the venerable oak's dappled shade
in the tranquillity of filigreed foliage,
mosaics of maples in bronze, copper and ochre,
a thousand and one shades of newly born green,

you will have a vision of heaven with all its munificence –
rhododendrons and azaleas, camellias and magnolias,
clusters of pink and red, mauve and purple, white and yellow.

If you can sit under the autumnal canopy on a mattress of leaves
as the afternoon sun refracts the rich, kaleidoscopic colours
and hear the excited voices of children blend in the breeze.

If you can listen to the sound of acorns falling,
worship the Japanese maples in crimson, gold and ruby,
flaming lanterns against the sombre yew at dusk –
you will be one with the universe, free.

AWAKENING

The red-breasted robin projected its greeting,
full throated to its mate on the arrival of spring.

The grey squirrel furtively posed for me with her paws,
balancing her loot, having already stuffed her jaws.

The frisky dog criss-crossing Highgate Wood
stopped for me as his mistress slowly jogged.

An old pensioner bent with age greeted
me with: Beautiful morning! We smiled,
and briefly stopped to acknowledge the gift.

The laughter of children cascaded upon us like church bells
as they space-walked into a golden enclosure,
their playground, balancing the sun in their voices.

The sky was blue against the startled deep-green of a tall
holly bush in a wood filled with naked, sun-drenched trees.

The spirit of the day kept growing upon me.
Carpe diem, carpe diem, carpe diem...
whispered the wind through the glass of time.

HIGHGATE WOOD

(for my aunts)

Unmistakable the freshness of fragrances
of pine, chestnut and honeysuckle,
welcoming as I enter by the Gypsy Gate,
revealing glimpses of a thousand and one faces.

A moment of jubilation when the sunlight
streams in, startling the plants growing
wild in their coppiced site, silhouettes
stretching and chasing each other in the bright
green meadow poised in the distance.

When the sun disappears,
leaving me with the knowledge piecemeal
of leaves and trees, daughters and mothers –

I wander into the woodland's womb
sprawling ancient earthwork,
seeking space to replenish myself
on the floor of this weeping cathedral.

The sun reappears nurturing creatures
bursting out of their cocoons,
negotiating a passage through the world –
the weakest learning to stand together,
the strong cherished in harmony.

The whistling and twittering of birds,
the spluttering of woodpeckers,
the wind-tickled chimes of a charm of finches
with the double rainbow renew hope.

Est, ergo cogito: It is, therefore I think.

We are what others make of us –
pearls in a necklace resplendent in company.

BOXING DAY

(for my uncles)

The full moon rose like an aria in the sky,
my thoughts, a flock of birds, heave homewards.

The landline hums with voices of my little nephews and nieces
assuring me all's well with the world –

their vowels travelling excitedly over
windswept clouds, buoyed across continents,
carrying the joy of the universe in their drift,
showering me with armful of gifts.

No longer cold and restless like the monkeys in the temple
of Jagannath, I let the snow scatter the darkness of my soul.

Through the window I stare at stars shining steadfastly.
All children are messengers of hope –

I remember the words of my grandfather
uttered in a moment of grace and lucidity.

Old age arrives with no warning,
bringing with it disease, dependence and suffering.

Crossing the boundary between human and divine,
my spirit swirls like music.

Christ, Krishna or Ganesha are as much my endowment
as all the children who sleep hungry tonight.

SHAADI.COM

My ideal partner would be someone like myself –
preferably never married, will settle for divorced
or widowed with children with the right chemistry.
Tall, dark, slim and romantic; must have a GSOH.

Kind, understanding, generous, loyal, trustworthy,
goes without saying. Financially, emotionally secure,
well-educated, thoughtful, a man of action he must be.
Non-smoker, occasional drinker, must enjoy good food,
but be prepared to eat anything unless he wants to cook.
Must like reading, travelling, have a passion for Life.
Religion? A Brahmin would be nice but not essential.

I wrapped my expectations with a neat summation:
Don't have a fixed idea of what I want, but know that
when we meet, I will know and so will he.

Having spent one balmy summer evening registering,
I decided to cool off with a glass of chilled champagne,
thinking of the beautiful boy doing his best in time.

But I received a response straight away:
No matches found; change your criteria, be realistic.

That my ideal man was not found was a blow, I confess.
It doesn't mean such a man does not exist,
I reasoned, pulling my self-esteem back into harness.
He is simply not registered with this agency!

Having determined to do something about it,
I persisted in my pursuit of Mr Almost Right.

Must try other agencies, cast my net wider;
meanwhile, no harm in checking out what's on offer,
be less fussy, let karma in on such a deep matter.

Age: Doesn't matter. Marital status: Doesn't matter.
Children: Doesn't matter. Country of residence: Doesn't matter.
Height: Doesn't matter. Education: Doesn't matter.
Religion: Doesn't matter. Occupation: Doesn't matter.
I was inundated with suitors, crashing my computer.

WISHES

Having tied strings on trees, walls, stones,
wished on the new moon, fallen eyelashes,
tossed coins in rivers, fountains, wells,
sometimes over my head and shoulder
in more places than I care to remember,

circled several times the sacred scarab,
climbed mountains, hugged pillars, statues;
kissed icons, shrouds, Shiva Linga,
images of gods, goddesses, saints;
          made donations,
fasted on different days of the week, prayed
to the sun, moon and other divine powers,
lighted candles in churches, cathedrals,
folded my palms in prayer in temples,
knelt reverently in mosques and pagodas –

I have learnt that wishes are milestones
          on our journey back home.
Nothing disappears without a trace,
only our pilgrimage transforms as we learn
to celebrate our brief passage with grace.

BEWARE

I

Beware of living in a nation
with no road signs or price tags in shops,
and certainly no Freedom of Information.

It could be a massive experiment in progress
by the rulers to improve verbal communication
as the government is bankrupt and its people illiterate.

It could also be that the people are simply super-intelligent,
psychic, lateral thinkers who excel in problem solving,
and instinctively know how to figure things out.

It possibly encourages enterprise and intelligence gathering
as individuals ferret out ways of bartering information.

It certainly keeps the economy flowing and prevents people
from knowing whether they are coming or going.

II

Beware of living in a nation
with a surfeit of street signs and price tags in shops,
but still no real Freedom of Information.

It could be a massive experiment in progress
by the rulers to discourage communication
among its citizens for fear of increasing social cohesion.

It could also be that the people lack intelligence,
always in need of nurture, someone to hold their hand
as they remain illiterate, prevented from figuring things out.

It discourages enterprise and any form of self-knowing,
engaged perpetually in information processing,
leaving little time and energy for thinking.

It keeps the economy flowing, gives people the illusion
they are in control of their lives, coolly coming and going.

EASTER MESSAGE

Swathed in a dirty shawl, embracing large bundles of plastic
bags like dead infants in her arms, she sits in the carriage
indifferent to the Underground destinations we tunnel through.

She speaks to herself in a language I fail to decipher.
Her direct gaze into my eyes reminds me of my mother.

Another commuter leans forward as if to answer her questions,
thinking she asked for directions, a foreigner lost in the Tube.

Life taught her never to depend on the kindness of strangers.

Her eyes are nomad, her words nonsense. He listens, she smiles.
For an instant they try to converse.

A refugee from Croatia, Kosovo or Albania, she is a survivor.

We hear the words, but do not understand her story.
She pauses briefly, chuckles on her fate
before she starts like a scratched record all over again.

I get off at Victoria, the carriage disgorges
itself and gets choked again. She sits there oblivious
to stations and announcements on the Circle Line.

DISPOSSESSED

We embarked on this pilgrimage
to the promised land beyond the treacherous seas,
true believers, steadfast in our faith.

Dreaming of placing trust
in an adopted homeland, thought
life would be no longer cheap, easily snatched.

Did not realize death had so many paths,
so many notions of justice or redemption.

We knew the islands were beautiful
when we stowed ourselves, leaving the rest to God,
praying to the Immortal to bring us here.

Our country is closed in, our days clouded by war.
At night fear rose like the moon,
spreading its shroud over death and hunger.

We came here believing in freedom,
believing if we wished it long and hard
our dreams would turn to truth.

We did not expect a miracle,
we did not look back –
have we not paid enough?

If you need more
take us,
whatever is left of our dreams, our possessions –
only spare our children, our future…

RETURN OF THE EXILE

We are all returning.
– *The Qur'an*

After years of wandering, I return
to this strange place, the home I left,
forgotten in the land of my birth.

Nourished under alien skies,
I come looking for certainties,
a child alone woken by nightmares,
unable to drift back to a land of dreams.

Gone is the mansion, the garden I grew up in,
gone are my people, landscape of my childhood.

None left here to comfort me
through the long journey into light
or nothingness, redemption or oblivion,
no compensation for turning back.

We have hardened ourselves, grown up –
no longer ask questions we do not understand.

Can't we explode space and time
back to when it all began,
demand to know why we were sent here,
why so hard the lives given to us,
some more than others?

Where do we go when our time is up,
our insignificant lives
tempered by the questions we ask?

BLACK SWANS

The highly expected not happening is also a Black Swan.

– *Nassim Nicholas Taleb*

Look into your own history –
exile from family, friends, country,
betrayed by those you placed your faith in,
always living at the margins.

Yet nothing, yes nothing in your past
pointed to the unfurling of the present.

What has been, what might have been –
two fractured landmasses drifting in time
acquiring individual perspectives,
not parallel lines meeting in infinity.

You wander down lanes of lives never lived,
reconciling what might have been with reality.

Is there free will? you ask as you sink,
failing to swim against the tide, knowing
only dead fish swim with the stream.

Immense possibilities only appear
to be evenly distributed; not knowing the odds
we take risks, act against the gods.

There is no way of knowing what we don't know.
No way of protecting us against uncertainty.

We build theories like terracotta armies,
fallible guesses from fragmentary information,
success or failure being always retrospective.

Our limitations echo in memory,
rearing up in dreams of the seemingly impossible,
our own lives, elegant black swans, in full flight...

THE WISHING TREE

Children conspiring around the ancient
tree trunk encircle it with their voices
clamouring to cover branches with tinsel –
calligraphically scripted dreams,
poems of love, coins at the bottom of a well,
prayer flags at monasteries
          along foothills of the Himalayas.

A father hoists his son on his shoulders
tall as he leans to tie a prayer on a wing.

Mother and daughter, hands outstretched
          cast dreams that spell the light:

If only I could walk
          in the hearts of my enemies...

Let father be able to speak again.
Let my sister regain her sight.

Let mother come home soon from hospital.
Let my brother who left home a year ago return.

Let me learn to love without limitation.
          Let there be peace in our lives.

May God hold us always
          in the palm of his hand...

GOING HOME

(for Doris Lessing)

Look after her, she is your responsibility...

You hear a stranger's voice –
small, personal, urgent – before vanishing,

and you watch over a child
miraculously brought into your care.

Life mere briefing for a descent into hell,
all part of a larger rhythm you can tell.

The sun lies at our feet in this four-gated city.
The wind blows away our words,
not the prisons we choose to live in.

Assume nothing, consider all sides,
things could easily have turned out differently.

Was it like this for you, too? she enquires,
recounting her childhood experiences.

Growing up is a place where everything's cracked,
nothing's permanent, no foundations solid.

You look at things from different angles,
lying in the grass singing, summer before the dark.

Every survivor needs a memoir, a golden notebook –
writing a habit of loving, like breathing.

All of us are shaped by war, twisted and warped,
our inner battles spilling out from under our skin.

From *Dreams That Spell the Light*

Our body, the old chief's country, landlocked –
like a proper marriage, a ripple from the storm.

Having known many homes, many dreams
you learn finally to live with the freedom of a spirit,
heart like a prairie field, open –

not the dispossession of one shut behind a door,
holding it ajar only to be greeted by desperate,
unceasing, silent screams.

THE DREAM

The road ends abruptly like an unfinished sentence,
no signposts, no explanation; a dirt road
washed away in the rain, in the middle of the night,
in the middle of nowhere with no one to guide me there.

The landscape is luminous, merging with a sky
showered with meteors, a celebration with fireworks.

I sit dazed in the car, locked like a jewel in a safe,
a garden enclosed, a sealed well,
waiting for someone to break into my solitude,
to disturb my peace, carry away the burden

held secret all these years –
except I can no longer remember what it is.

IT

Before you turn the page, start reading *it* –
That's it. That started it. It is. Goes on. Moves. Beyond.
Becomes. Becomes it and it and it. Goes further than that...

You are mesmerized by the cover.
A world has come into the world within the world –
the world in your hands is for your pleasure.

You discover something new about yourself,
start seeing in a new light. Is *it*

a tree with branches, a dried leaf on canvas,
a negative print of an extraordinary shot of it
with the full moon's whiteness
clustering at the edges like fat on meat?

Is it backlit by the sun, an orgasmic
piercing light penetrating the picture?

Is it an image of a cross section of the brain?
You overhear a stranger ask another –
gasping with wonder at the possibilities
of *it*, of life, matter, anti-matter, non-matter?

We give and take according to our measure,
open-ended our interpretation of things.

Imagine the surprise when you learn
the cover photograph is mud flat at low tide,
photograph taken on 15 April 1944
courtesy of the Royal Canadian Air Force.

From *Dreams That Spell the Light*

And your journey begins through everything –

Language that is water, air, light, earth,
shining nerves spread out like angel wings;
sun in water shimmering, the aura of kings,
earth a mirror for what cannot be seen.

SOMEWHERE, SOMETHING

We travel not to explore another country,
but to return home fresh, bearing gifts.

Our lives the airports we fly from,
our bodies and souls, maps and compasses –
days the journeys we make,
past the continents we leave behind.

Surely there is somewhere, something
that justifies our coming and going?

Isn't that why we seek a sign from each other
of experiences worth dying for
as we commune with love under starlight
brittle with frost and the sharp taste of blood?

Let's fly free, not nailed to a mast;
see the universe with new eyes,
not blinded by shadows that light casts.

Imagine

New Poems

For life, art, friendship – all who made this journey possible

To know is nothing at all; to imagine is everything.

–*Albert Einstein*

What is now proved was once only imagined.

–*William Blake*

I do not know how to distinguish between our waking life and a dream. Are we not always living the life that we imagine we are?

–*Henry David Thoreau*

I am the life of everything to come.

–*Mahabharata*

LADDER OF ESCAPE

(for Joan Miro)

A time for retreat
to a world imagined
perhaps a river made iridescent
by the passage of a swan
a time to rise above
the incompleteness of life
embrace emptiness
invisibility liberation
discover rays of opportunity
wander in ecstasy
guided by tracks of tortoises
plunge into anonymity
that final flight into the light
a cosmic web of stars
caressing the breast of happiness
casting off cobwebs of prejudices
prisons built by us our past selves
drawing with smoke on air
magical things written on the heart
tree of life with ears and eyes
dewdrops trembling in surprise
language beyond grief and joy
prophetic a ladder of escape.

AMONG THE IMMORTALS

I dream my painting and I paint my dream.

– *Vincent van Gogh*

Reflecting on life's many false starts –
art dealer, teacher, lover, preacher – always the outsider,
fearful of failure, loss of face, faith, family,
except for brother Theo providing a reason for living
in sorrow yet ever joyful.

In the depths of darkness,
moments of clarity bridge the gap between art and reality.
Dwelling in possibility, awareness of the one true God
gives way to insight – quest for the light within all beings.

The idea at first vague until the initial impulse,
a scribble, takes form, becomes a sketch
and the sketch a painting – mastery of the thing
promising an unexpected flowering.

Brushstrokes come alive in a rapture of aseity,
crying out with creations of flesh and blood –
self-portraits breathing, original in their view of the infinite,
touch the heart of humanity, open a door to eternity,
walk among the immortals, communing with the light.

L'ATELIER ROUGE

(After *The Red Studio*, a painting by Henri Matisse)

You painted this studio a radiant scarlet –
a luminous sunset
spreading joy with increasing abandonment.
The glass is empty, not your plate.

Absorbed in your creations I wait,
thinking you will walk in any moment,
start sharing stories of paintings on paintings,
remind me that creativity takes courage.

Uncovering the blue and yellow beneath the red,
I note the walls were white,
you changed the colours until they felt right.

Your signature is everywhere,
the way you fit things to make a whole.

While working you *never try to think, only feel*
and connect – woman and man, earth and sky,
tree like a human body, human body like a cathedral,
studio like a private universe. Art the only thing
that matters once it stops hurting.

The green blue light of the window
intensifies the interior where memory
is suspended like the grandfather clock
whose face has no hands –
the fathomless mirror reflects no illusions.

An open box of crayons offers paradise
contained in this world within worlds of yours,
teaching me how to lose and find myself in art.

WHAT DOES IT MEAN?

Walking into an art retrospective
with carcasses of a calf, gold-plated hooves and horns,
bull, zebra, sheep, shark, unicorn floating in formaldehyde –
the unicorn is called *The Dream*.

The Dream Is Dead when the unicorn is cast in solid silver.
Here is art proclaiming *The Physical Impossibility of Death*
in the Mind of Someone Living.

A painting of four skulls transforms itself into
Beautiful Artemis Thor Neptune Odin Delusional Sapphic
Inspirational Hypnosis.

Just when *You start to think you are touched by God*,
For the Love of God consider yourself a *possibilian*,
there are whispers about money, investments –
someone asks: *Darling, what does it mean*?

You mean *The Acquired Inability to Escape*?
a voice moves like steel on glass, *In and Out of Love*.

You spin on a table, *Loving in a World of Desire*.
The Last Thing I Said to You was Don't Leave Me Here.

We move on to *Black Sun*, clusters of dead flies,
Beautiful Inside My Head Forever
diamonds meticulously arranged like pills

Thirty Pieces of Silver, *Cold Dark Matter: An Exploded View*, pornographic drawings
and a yard screaming with sculptures put together
from fresh food, cigarette butts, tights, crushed objects,
wood shavings…

TIME UNCOVERING TRUTH

Home to nudes in painting and sculpture,
the gossip in this country of art and culture

is about a government cover-up, plain and simple –
not the credit crunch or corruption, but a missing nipple.

Image consultants in the prime minister's office obsessed
with a bare breast, voluptuous and self-possessed –

Tiepolo's *Time Uncovering Truth* backdrop for every press
conference caught on camera alongside the PM's face.

Out of touch with public sentiment they repainted the lady's gown
just to cover the offending bosom. Young men about town

joined art critics in pronouncing the decision totally crazy,
called the government morally bankrupt and intellectually lazy.

Women protested by showing off their cleavage and more.
Aspiring artists gathered in galleries professing to explore

the skill and ingenuity involved in the delineation of breasts.
Cartoonists had fun with impotent politicians' hairless chests.

Clueless foreign tourists received free master classes
on the integrity of naked human bodies by instructors in glasses.

In every street posters of Madonna and Child, milk squirting
from her bust, hung in protest. It's just a misunderstanding,

confessed a senior source from the Ministry of Culture; story
was the PM ordered the painting be restored to its original glory.

Tongues wagged with pleasure as reporters gathered to admire
the infamous nipple and breast. Frankly, rest of the news was dire!

MAKING THINGS RIGHT

(for Benny Goodman)

When it came to things that mattered
he never compromised –
never forgot his father slaving
away in stockyards, shovelling
lard, coming home in those boots
exhausted, stinking.

He kept searching for reasons
for his untimely demise,
why some lives are harder than others.

His parents had risked everything.
This was no time to stop dreaming
of making things right,
stop grieving for all that was lost, endured.

It was the gift of music that set him free.

Refusing to be fenced in by segregation,
he created music that knew no boundaries –
almost bringing down the Iron Curtain.

Everyone began to jitterbug to the ritzy rhythms,
swooning women wanted him to do to them
what he did with music:

Sing, Sing, Sing, *Life Goes to a Party*...
When My Baby Smiles at Me,
Sometimes I'm Happy, Don't Be That Way...
The glitzy razzmatazz of jazz left them giddy.

When love entered his dreams, chatting, listening,
he proposed to her with music plucked out
of his clarinet, a trembling wedding ring.

SAXOPHONE COLOSSUS

He moves centre-stage
            a grizzled silverback –
legendary leader of his band. Tenor madness
grips the audience, makes them swoon.

Saxophone colossus swings to the music,
gathering a strong syncopated beat,
hypnotizing us with his wry, nimble wit,
his lion's roar and explorer's heart.

The sinewy hard-bop, uplifting ballads, saucy calypsos
and soul jazz declare: *I'm one of the last guys left…*
Last of the devils dancing with a tune in his head.

As the musicians jam, breathless –
the percussionist's face changes contour,
mouth opening, closing like a tilapia's. The guitar,

trombone, bass players turn into mythical creatures,
conjuring sounds from secret planets – notes
ephemeral, eternal, never experienced before.

The blonde drummer in his saffron dress
is a Buddhist monk beating his path to happiness –
their improvisations carry us to states unknown.

The tenor saxophone, an extension of his doubled-up
body bent to the ground, challenging evolution,
        draws the last orgasmic gasps.

THE LAST DANCE

When doubt dances in your mind like a devil,
twists your reason, plays with memory until
you forget the familiar face of love, no longer feel
the gentle hand protecting you, guiding the world
with its goodness, the way waves polish shells on the beach.

Suddenly water gets sprayed on your face, lips laced with salt –
Margarita kiss. You find yourself in Caesar's Palace,
gambling your fortune, friends, family with funny
money, credit swaps, sub-prime mortgages, offshore accounts.

Nobody asks you any questions, nor do you take stock
of your naked positions. The house of cards collapses –
you know you've been skewered, left roasting on a spit.

When doubt lands inside you like a bumblebee,
descending down the throat of flowers, humming in the dark,
drunk with honey, dazzled, dusting off pollen,
you lose your sense of purpose in the universe.

Nothing left to return home to. Faith, hope, love – all gone.
Dispossessed, you daren't deny the Devil the last dance.

FLAMENCO

What is this dance that turns a woman to fire?
– *Rainer Maria Rilke*

Her entry lights up the dark stage –
a flame shuddering in rich shades of autumn,
the sun rising on a sea of crimson.

Smouldering black eyes hold secrets
buried deep in the earth for centuries.

Lightning glances dart back and forth, her smiles
sparkle with flashes of diamonds and rubies.

Life flows through her limbs, speaking
of love and betrayal, death and redemption.

Music moves to the rhythm of her singing feet,
arms sway like snakes coupling –
the world whirls on her fingertip.

The clapping of hands and clacking of castanets
rise in a crescendo of applause –
the crowd enthralled cheer for more.
Mesmerized, they watch her feet, arms, hips, lips.

Flicking her wrist, spinning her skirt,
her face framed by the night of her coiled hair,
she swirls in a frenzy, leaving us giddy.

A blazing inferno circles her with cries
of admiration. Her feet draw a drumroll –
with a gesture of disdain she tames the fire,
          stamping out the illusion.
Lights dim, darkness descends...

DILEMMA

When Ustad Sahib was invited to appear
on Desert Island Discs, it was an honour

he reckoned, but felt compelled to consider
the constraints of such an offer.

The songs I came to sing remain unsung,
the words I wait for, the notes, elude me.

There stirs in me a kind of restlessness.
I have symphonies to create, destinies to fulfil.

The music that lives in me was conceived
before the beginning of time.

How do I bare my soul in eight compositions,
a couple of minutes each?

What about a live audience? One cannot recreate
in a vacuum, even the magic of Krishna's flute

was inspired by his growing circle of gopis.
Music shared with others grows within us.

Orpheus charmed wild beasts,
brought stones to life with his harmonies.

Kalidasa communicated with clouds,
bringing down the heavens with his melodies.

Earth and sky are my canvas.
Time, the keeper of secrets, my trusted teacher.

Life, my muse, keeps her rainbow window open,
a mirror that shatters itself hearing music.

WONDER OF THE AGE

He had seen emperors come and go –
some rising to giddy pinnacles of wealth and power
only to be imprisoned, murdered.
But a true artist never lacked work.

A painter of saints, holy men and gods,
he knew all about creation.
Each time he painted a living being,
etched every bone, nerve, muscle and limb,
he could never breathe life into the image.
Made him marvel at the miracle wrought
by the Supreme Artist – the universe
an expression of the divine imagination.

As a child he learnt how to chisel paintbrushes
from quills of birds, setting them with fine hairs
plucked from kittens and baby squirrels.
He sorted minerals, grain by grain –
carnelian, malachite, lapis-lazuli and emeralds,
according to their purity and brilliance,
each stone a prayer speaking in colours.

Other pigments he made from insects, metals,
earth and animal matter, the world
his canvas and palette, a rainbow of desire –
for a cool yellow gold he added silver,
for a warmer hue he used copper,
learning to master the art of making gold glitter.
Early in life, he had the honour
of receiving the royal title, Wonder of the Age.

Sitting on a kelim, one arthritic knee flexed
to support his drawing board, his paintbrush connecting
him with everything. His loneliness dissolving,
he wondered: Is this how God feels?

PAINTER OF GODS

I

It takes five days for the spirit of the gods
to descend, for the readiness of the canvas –

from soaking the tamarind seeds in water,
grinding it to a thick pulp in a mortar,

stirring the paste on a gentle fire
until left with a residue, the glue

to stick two layers of cloth, cotton or tussar,
before buffing it with the fine powder

of the soft clay stone from the Nilgiri mountains
that lends the piece its unique colour.

Once dried in the sun it is cut and polished
with a semi-precious stone,

then with a smooth pebble or piece of wood.
I've followed this ritual since my childhood.

First one must bathe and pray in the temple,
be pure of body, mind and soul.

The highest good is lending our lives
to the mystery and majesty of God's purpose.

Imagine the universe when it was nothing,
awaiting the imprint of the divine imagination.

What would it be like if we could live each moment
as a masterpiece in the throes of creation?

II

Father taught me all about colour –

conch shells for white, lamp soot for black,
yellow from the hartala stone, vermillion from cinnabar,

green a gift from the leaves of the neem tree,
blue from indigo and the khandaneela stone.

We made paintbrushes with keya root,
the finer brushes with carved wooden handles

have mouse hair. A dozen long hairs at the centre
give it a needle-point edge when dipped in paint.

Tracing our ancestors back to the eighth century,
when the painting of patta-chitras as souvenirs

for pilgrims turned into a profession,
and the craft was passed down generations,

father instilled in me a hunger for perfection.
A work of art is true worship of the divine.

He saw me as the village's first female master-painter.
My parents wished for a son, which family doesn't?

When mother died giving birth to one,
he never took another woman, called me his treasure and son.

It is my turn to keep alive the tradition –
what does it matter if I am a woman?

MEETING SHIVA AND PARVATI

(In the British Museum)

Meandering like a river
among the exhibits I encounter
Shiva and Parvati engrossed in each other,
holding the universe between their eyes.

Startled to find an offering of flowers,
nestling at their feet where
Nandi, Shiva's bull, and Parvati's lion
gaze bashfully at each other,
this statue from Orissa, the place of my birth
carved between AD 1100–1300
on gleaming black schist demands my attention.

I am in the presence of God
conceived as a couple, male and female,
on the point of becoming One.

Over two centuries have elapsed
since the divine pair –
dressed lavishly in decorated loincloths,
their naked bodies adorned with ornaments
earrings, necklaces, headdresses, anklets –

were taken from their home in an ornate temple,
perhaps in Bhubaneswar, the abode of gods,
where worshippers thronged for a darshan
offering gifts and prayers,
holding conversations with gods that began in
the temple and were carried on every day, everywhere.

Here, the gods sit silently contemplating the world
and each other, oblivious of a broken-hearted believer.
Have you forgotten your daughter, how long must I suffer
alone buffeted by life's crosswinds before I find shelter?

SWIMMING REINDEER

(After *Swimming Reindeer*: Sculpture carved from mammoth tusk, found in Montastruc, France 11,000 BC. British Museum, London)

Slim, compact, slightly curved, carved
from the tapering end of a mammoth's tusk –
a female reindeer decorated with incised lines,
the male with an imposing set of antlers
folded along the length of his back.

Chins up, antlers tipped back, they swim
legs stretched, bodies' streamlined, bones breathing
unable to sleep for being alive –
their pristine presence a shaft of light.

Not created for any religious ceremony,
not a love charm, this sculpture
with no known functional purpose
conjures an image of a herd of reindeer,
roaming across colourless, treeless plains
in an Ice Age where time does not stand still,
sprints like a hunter intent on surviving
in an unforgiving planet.

The skill of the toolmaker turned artist,
was it one or many,
evokes a vision of grace, of faces rapt in wonder,
fingers chiselling, bone folded on bone, in prayer,
a desire to be at home in the universe –
a reaching out when nature rewired the brain
and the world lit up like aurora borealis.

HUNGER

The gecko's progress across the ceiling,
its scaly limbs defying gravity,
eyes fixed on its prize, hypnotized,
is matched by the speckled moth's nervous
fluttering against the fluorescent bar light.

I too watch mesmerized, waiting for a taxi
to take me to the Siddhivinayak Temple.

The wildlife programme on TV
hones in on a cheetah chasing a gazelle,
the cheetah swiftly walks away with its kill.

A neighbour's dog barks drunkenly
as I walk past the entrance to a consumptive car.

Dark, sunken, famished eyes peer at me
behind the closed, tinted window screens
each time the car slows at traffic lights –
long enough for mother and child to gesture
for alms, palms rising in salaam.

When I hand out ten rupees, my car is
mobbed with a hundred hungry eyes.

Across the road a life-sized poster sells dreams.
An actor gazes enchanted into the eyes
of his beloved, lips barely touching.

In the temple an emaciated devotee
crawls across the tarmac penitent for his sins –
a caterpillar crossing from leaf to leaf,
declaring eternal hunger for His love and mercy.

I join the evening queue for darshan,
my hands laden with flowers, earthen lamp, offerings.

It is Divine hunger, this Creation…
I overhear a conversation about Darwin and evolution,
dark matter, origin of the universe, religion,
Einstein, Hadron Collider and the Magician,
the meaning of life, Higgs Boson,
in answer to the question: What is maya, illusion?

YOU

When I was lost you came to my rescue.
I wanted to thank you, but could not see you.
Not knowing what you looked like, I called you –
by all your names, the ones I knew.
Hearing my cries the wind whispered in my ear
thousands of your names. I could not remember
them, but my desire to meet you grew.
Travelling through time and space, learning
of ways in which your name's been defiled,
my anger turned into a flame. I wondered why you
tolerate so much injustice, is that your way too?
My thoughts fixed on you, I caught glimpses of you
everywhere; heard stories of your coming and going.
When you changed form I changed mine too,
the force of illusion carrying me through,

though always destined to miss you.
When I reached the limit of my disguises –
knowing only you are without limitation
and not knowing one's limitation a human
predilection – I was lost. Lost in you.

KNOWING INFINITY

An equation for me has no meaning unless it expresses
a thought of God.

– *Ramanujan*

The pilgrimage from Erode – wet skull,
land of legends and gods, where an enraged
Shiva tore off one of Brahma's five heads –
and Kumbakonam – where touched
by smallpox at the age of two, refusing
to speak till three, losing younger siblings
to disease and death, you left your child-wife
with your mother already struggling to make
ends meet and your father going blind –

your journey from the familiar sounds
of the Cauvery, the temple bells of Namakkal
and fervent prayers to stone deities –
to the hallowed quads and corridors of Trinity,
(when India was British and Victoria still Queen),
the silent mists of Cam, church bells, choir in chapel,
Gothic windows and cloisters of Whewell's Court –

a place strange, stone cold, distant, indifferent
to everything you lived for, believed in –
is a tale from the ancient Hindu epics
where gods changed the course of human lives.
Did the power of your deity weaken
beyond the seven seas?

In Cambridge your world
was turned upside down, inside out –
faced with prejudice and rejection,
lonely and malnourished, unable to return home,
caught in a war that landed at your doorstep
with its sick and injured. In the middle of all this
you were diagnosed with tuberculosis.

For five years you struggled, sought solace
in the truths of mathematics,
made friends with fractions, integers, algorithms.

Born with a quick mind, your thoughts
travelling with the speed of light,
you assumed your peers would keep up,
not shoot down your flights of intuition,
demand proof of your conclusions,
examine the black box of your equations –

unable to decipher the hieroglyphics
of your imagination, the great Unknown your life
was etched on, art created in a language of symbols –
your inspiration, dancing gods, rejoicing in
spaces infinitesimally large and small.

Even your greatest champion
could not keep pace with your soaring insights –
the things you could see a mystery to others.

With unlimited faith in your gift,
you sacrificed everything – family, home, love, life…

Did you have premonitions of your demise,
a premature death at the age of thirty-two –
know there was not a moment to waste
in transcribing the legacy of a lifetime?

Did you know that anything less –
the least bit less confidence in your ability,
dedication, persistence, patience or luck,
would consign you to obscurity?

What were the odds of you not being
remembered as the man who knew infinity?

SPRING FEVER

(After a painting, *Yogini in the forest*, Ashmolean Museum, Oxford)

It must have something to do with the air,
not the avocado, asparagus, oysters,
figs with almonds and honey, the dark chocolate
they had for lunch, he thought absent-mindedly,
admiring a pretty young thing peering
ardently at an ethereal portrait of a female ascetic
in a forest somewhere in India, centuries past,
having renounced the world, its ecstasy, its suffering.

Both women, hair tied back in a tight bun on the head,
appear absorbed in a silent conversation –
one heart no longer yearning after earthly pleasures.
The yogini's body bare except for a loincloth,
plain earrings, necklace, and a prayer band.

She sits alone in splendid possession
of herself, framed in a golden
halo of light, holding a rosary.
The stream in the foreground is adorned
with lotus flowers, leaves levitate
like inverted emerald-thalis, worshipping
alongside a pair of ducks pecking and preening.

The five trees in the background stand
to attention, their rich foliage contained
like her wild senses, her leopard-skin seat
signifying the conquest of her animal self.

As he disrobes her in his mind – she already
clad scantily like the lady in the painting –
the boyfriend arrives. They kiss and hug hungrily.
Absorbed in each other they walk away, whispering.

COOK AND THE CHICKPEA

(With acknowledgement to Rumi)

A chickpea leaping out of the pot,
no more dry and hard, but ready to sprout,
soaked overnight, then boiled fiercely,
yelled with all its might at the cook:
Why are you doing this to me?

The cook, casting the chickpea back in the pot,
as if guiding a whale stranded on the beach,
breathless and lost, back into the ocean, replied:

When will you stop thinking
only about yourself, begin to accept my cooking,
careful and constant, as your destiny?

How am I torturing you when all I am doing
is enriching your bland goodness with spices,
salt, garlic, ginger, turmeric and tomatoes,
so you can mix with rice and vegetables,
and nourish my master's family?

Remember the way you were tended
as you drank rain in my master's garden, doing
nothing, feeding on minerals and other nutrients?

You have come a long way from a seed
planted in the vegetable garden
to the dawn of a new life in a cooking pot,
to a taste conjured by me specially for you,
providing nourishment to humans.

Don't you know we are all returning,
our lives enriched by serving,
our home where we are going?

EURYDICE'S STORY

I

Inconsolable at her loss – parts of Orpheus' body buried in Mount Olympus, his head in the island of Lesbos – Eurydice pleaded for her release from Hades so she could give Orpheus a decent burial. Not knowing how to prepare for such an adventure, Eurydice sought the counsel of Savitri.

'It was simple for me,' said the pure one. 'I could not take my eyes off Satyavan, followed him everywhere until Yama gave in to my requests. Talk to Isis, you have so much in common.' Savitri led Eurydice to Krishna who emanated divine melody perched on a tree with branches draped in colourful saris billowing skywards, tugging like trapped kites.

Are all the lovers of the world musicians of sorts? Eurydice mused as she smiled at the half-naked maidens of Mathura frolicking in the pond camouflaged beneath the old gnarled canopy of the ancient tree, unashamedly rejoicing. Krishna's breath was music, he exhaled Om, oblivious of the women clamouring after him, his face serene, smiling. Pity Orpheus did not learn a few of these tricks, thought Eurydice, drawn to this dark-blue boy who charmed the gopis, kept Radha and all his wives happy. When Krishna finally let the silence of the universe in, Eurydice's question – 'Krishna, how can I bring Orpheus back to life?' – danced in the wind. He spoke of human limitation, illusion, the soul's eternal quality, etc. Just when Eurydice thought she was getting the drift of Krishna's meaning he disappeared from her sight.

II

Eurydice carried on with her journey, visited the Palace of Isis where the Queen sat absorbed, listening to songs of the Nile: *Come water of life that flows from heaven. The sky burns, earth trembles at the coming of God. The mountains to the east, the mountains to the west make way preparing for the arrival of the One who takes possession of Egypt.*

On seeing Eurydice, Isis rose from her meditation, welcomed her guest, a tragic figure of grief, travel-fatigued. In the Queen's private chamber they poured their hearts out. 'I am so sorry to hear of your misfortune,' consoled Isis. 'My life has also been hard. While Osiris, my dearest husband and God-king, was away in the East, Mesopotamia to be precise, doing his kingly duties, his brother was planning royal treachery. Seth lured my husband into a trap and slew Osiris, usurped his throne, scattered his limbs across Egypt.' At this point both women started weeping uncontrollably, holding hands, kissing, embracing. 'It was devastating searching for his remains. With faithful Anubis's help we recomposed Osiris's body. Then a miracle occurred the day my tears fell on him – like the tears of heaven that keeps this land alive.'

The rest as they say is history. Osiris ascended to heaven, not before giving Isis the gift of their son, Horus, who took up the task started by his father after years of struggle with his uncle, the usurper.

III

Sitting at the feet of the Oracle in Lesbos, Eurydice asked herself: Why was I born so unlucky? Her time to return to Hades was imminent, her dream of finding Orpheus unfulfilled. The villagers had dug wide and deep at the feet of the hallowed mountain of Olympus, searching for fragments of any human body. They were disappointed of exploding yet another myth. Eurydice despaired of finding Orpheus, of ever going back to the way things were or might have been. She was beginning to get the drift of Krishna's meaning…

Mere hints and guesses – no oracles, no certainty. Life itself capricious and unforgiving, offering its gifts indiscriminately. Having reached her limit, her body unused to such harsh conditions, Eurydice accepted bread and wine from a stranger who reminded her of Orpheus, sometimes of Krishna and Osiris. At times she thought of him as Everyman, then there were times he reminded her of no one in particular.

Unafraid, she followed him into a field of light, the precipice of her being, ready to leap into the unknown. She had never trusted any man like that before. No longer sure of anything – it did not matter if she was in heaven, on earth, half-awake, half-dreaming – moving deeper into uncertainty, she was a bird in flight buoyed by uplifting currents of music.

RED

Lips   blushing cheeks
colour of magic   hennaed hands and feet
desire blazing like autumnal leaves

Fields of poppies   bouquet of roses
flowers of the gulmohur tree   flame of the forest
red hibiscus   fuchsia   roses   peonies
pomegranate seeds scattering like rubies

Red Cross for neutrality
blood bank   people dying of disease   wounded in war
red in heraldry   revolution   red light   red flag
danger signal   red light district   brothel
caught red handed   red faced like a monkey

Red button in the Mandarin's cap
ruby   coral   garnet   quartz   cornelian
red cap   revolutionist   bohemian
red tincture   philosopher's stone
Judas' red hair   Beefeater man
red herring   Red Sea   Red Indian

Shades of red in earth   sky   sunrise   sunset
cherries   carrots   chillies   tomatoes   beetroot
red blooded man   anaemic woman   haemoglobin
iron   menses   maternity ward   operation theatre
red rags   red capes   bullfights
countries in the red   secrets   red tape
red box of the Chancellor of the Exchequer

Mary in maroon-red and blue   *The Annunciation*
Marilyn Monroe   *Niagara*   Julia Roberts   *Pretty Woman*
Red carpet   caviar   Ferraris   Havana cigars
Indian weddings   red Benarasi silk saris
red bangles   sankha   vermillion on the forehead

blood on the sheets   red letter day   blood on the streets
love letters written in blood   rudraksha beads
Christ on the Cross   prayer flags   precious gifts.

THE SCREAM

Walking down the hill in the mystic light of autumn
surrounded by nature's vast and ageless kingdom,
in thrall to the city's sprawl, stretching to the skyline
I hear a sound, a voice primeval, half-human,
a cry of compassion, a song of survival,
music of the universe, mirror reflecting the soul.
The sun was setting in an ocean of blood, the crimson
horizon heaving. Clouds, birds, trees, all nature
hummed in unison as a scream ran through creation –
an orgasmic gasp, a howl of inexplicable origin,
like silence before the beginning of consciousness.
Time's scroll of suffering unfurled in a chorus of pain,
rising to a stillness – centuries of prayers for justice.
Darkness descended, the scream sighed: *I am existence*.

WALL OR WINGS

A wall is an idea defining the limit of our perception.
Our skin is a living wall, each cell pulsating with vision,

tells us who we are. Invisible walls protect us.
The earth's atmosphere wraps it in a shawl of gases.

It is not for nothing homes need walls, niches, arches,
doors, windows for dreams, laughter, disappointments.

Walls within walls are pilgrim souls, keeper of secrets.

Walls revel in disguises, come in many shapes and sizes,
prefer to remain anonymous, take several aliases.

Being a wall means perpetually adjusting your vision,
yet a wall is never beyond redemption.

When a wall lies between you and your dreams,
turn it into something else, let it take wings.

NIRBHAYA

Do not ask if I dare to dream
of a land where I can walk free, without fear,
the sacrifices made to flicker in that flame
of hope. Did not know the price would be so dear.

Life is a gift I thought, did not expect
it to be cheap, callously plucked – half-chewed
bones tossed drunkenly after the feast.

In the night of the splintering womb
my dreams turned into nightmares.

No mountain could carry my grief, no ocean
wash away my shame, no wind dry my tears.

Do not ask how many times I touched the heart
of grief prised open like a pomegranate,
my seeds spilling like rubies.
This is no time to forgive and forget.

Battered and broken, no hope of being mended,
my sorrow speaks in myriad voices, will not be silenced
till the sacrilege of rape and violence is atoned.

How long must we suffer, burn like incense,
hold on to faith, dreaming of change?
We have an entire universe to rearrange.

After centuries of dreaming we are awake, alive,
know what holds us together when things fall away.

As long as I can summon the strength to pick myself
up when cast in the gutter, and rise like a phoenix –
I'll let the universe know it does not exist without my dreams.

NATURE STUDIES

Why does a crab in the swamps of Bangladesh
need a tiger, the Brazil nut tree a rare orchid

and an agouti? Why does a gecko in Kenya need a giraffe,
a Canadian lynx a moth caterpillar?

They depend on each other! Children playing in the garden
proclaimed in a chorus, they were studying nature.

The task, mutually agreed, was to find a creature each,
dead or alive. Neatly displayed on a bench lay

a worm, frog, centipede, beetle, ladybird –
dead, wrapped in leaves, ready for burial.

Why does a ladybird crawl when it can fly?
The youngest asked, crying inconsolably.

It was a relief they had not yet learnt of giant harpy
eagles carrying off capuchin monkeys for dinner,

of herons gobbling up snakes, crocodiles munching
sharks, and polar bears eating their own cubs.

How long before they discover the darkly menacing
face of nature – killer whales wave washing

seal cubs, carnivorous forests fertilised by dead fish,
the necrophilia of penguins, man-eating tigers cruising for prey?

IMAGINE

The song of humpbacked whales,
breath of life flowing through conch shells,

uniquely decorated flukes falling on waves,
huge white flippers slapping the water.

Imagine a grizzly bear on its haunches
in the bend of the river scooping up silver slivers,
tossing minnows into its yawning mouth.

Forests, canyons, rivers, waterfalls, double rainbows,
the laughter of lightning holding us in thrall.

Blush of a bride, the sky at sunrise, sunset,
spreading in wild abandonment.

Imagine cloud formations of changing configurations,
dove white to crow black, altocumulus to tornado chasers.

Smile of a camel filling the loneliness of a desert,
a cheetah in motion, the dance of King Cobras.

Sighing of leaves when the wind gives them a shake,
hawks soaring on tides of air, wild wings streamlined.

A colony of bats singing, meditating upside down
on an ancient tree grown large as a grandparent.

The majesty of a reclusive snow leopard disappearing
in a blizzard on the slopes of Mount Everest.

A smoking volcano blowing spectacular hoops
of fire, pouring molten lava for days,
depositing ash on the tray of land.

Imagine a stately cavalcade of moving mountains of ice
in the Arctic, shimmering with the aurora borealis.

Brightly coloured wings of a butterfly hovering,
their translucency in moonlight revealing…

Now open your eyes wide and imagine
our rich world bereft of nature's blessing.

ASHOKA

I

By the time his father, King Bindusara, died,
the land between the two seas and beyond –

from Indus to Ganga, central Asia and Himalayas
to the southern tip of India – thundered

with chariots gleaming in the sun, their white
pennants proclaiming the power of the mighty Mauryas.

His grandfather, Chandragupta the Great,
achieved what Alexander conceded in defeat –

a formidable empire. Only one state remained
hostile, unbowed. Renowned for its trade routes by land

and sea – with its rich, representative, pluralistic tradition –
Kalinga was the missing jewel in Ashoka's crown.

This affluent, fertile and independent nation
needed to be taught a lesson, annexed to his dominion.

In the ninth year of his kingship Kalinga was conquered –
a hundred and fifty thousand people were deported.

Another hundred thousand Kalingans slaughtered,
many times that number perished in a bloody encounter.

The river Daya turned crimson after the massacre,
torched fields of crops blazed like a sacrificial yajna.

From dawn to dusk the wind sighed with the river
and the red earth where courage had defended honour.

The outraged sky screamed in silent tongues of fire
until it turned dark as the moon blocked out the sun.

Even the gods could not countenance such a disaster,
gathering from all the worlds to redress the matter.

Surveying the aftermath of his victory –
flourishing cities reduced to charnel pits of misery

with stinking corpses, bodies mutilated, villages burnt,
where women, children, even animals fled on seeing a stranger –

this heartless warrior, scourge of his enemies, warmonger,
contemptuously called Chandashoka long before the carnage

in Kalinga, whose ruthlessness was feared alike
by friends and foe, experienced deep remorse:

What have I done? If this is victory, what's defeat?

II

Wandering disguised in his ravaged realm,
his horse's hooves muffled by gods of the underworld,

the sunken eyes of children, fatherless and naked,
with bloated stomachs, scavenging the streets like wild

beasts whipped Ashoka's conscience the way he'd punished
his generals if they displayed in battle any sign of fear.

Unconcealed the disdain for his portly appearance,
short and squat, in the silent stares of the oppressed.

His eyes, previously feral as a hawk's, free of mercy,
were now tired, having seen too much suffering.

Stalked by the unflinching look in the eyes of a bhikhu –
young, blameless, flogged senseless, left to perish in prison –

hounded by the screams and curses of grieving widows,
the wheezing and begging of wizened old men,

the plight of young women left to fend for their families,
girls with no prospect of finding suitable husbands,

and terror like a mask frozen on the faces of carcasses,
haunted his dreams. Ashoka could not stop grieving:

Have I destroyed another country's splendour,
sacrificed the bravest and the best in an unholy war?

Have I ruined families to spend my days in hell?
Am I like these vultures and scavengers a messenger of evil?

Did I do this for prosperity, an empire, or vanity?
Was it greed for power that drove me to such insanity?

Is this victory or defeat, justice or injustice?
No good can ever come from hatred and vengeance.

Like waves in the ocean his doubting mind
would not be calmed, kept churning incessantly.

Ashoka, he who is without sorrow or pain,
having welded the wealth of the world into an empire

was transformed by dukkha, grief born of devastation
inflicted on a prosperous, peaceful and proud nation.

Ashoka Bindusara Maurya, Samraat Chakravartin,
Universal Emperor, saw in victory the cadaverous face

of defeat. Determined to repent, he resolved to renounce
violence, embrace Dhamma, rule as an enlightened king.

III

Born to rule, the path to becoming a Siddhartha –
he who achieves his aim, masters the meaning

of *Being* in every breath, thought, word and action –
was harder than returning triumphant from battle.

Ashoka knew of Gautama Buddha who at birth had also
lost his mother. The illustrious Gautama renounced everything –

his right to the throne, the palace where he was denied nothing.
The prince left his family, shaved his head, embraced poverty.

Declaring himself a sanyasin, he went seeking alms
in the streets of the ancient capital of Magadha,

hoping to earn the gift of suffering to see the light,
for the blind of illusion to lift, veil that distorts our sight.

Ashoka never forgot his father, King Bindusara,
the slayer of enemies, who mindful of his duty,

knowing no warrior ever went begging in the streets,
on hearing of Prince Gautama's spiritual quest

offered his throne to the prince. The seeker
of truth, his mind on higher things, chose prayer,

self-discipline, right action – release from reincarnation
requiring the surrender of all ambition.

Tired of getting what he wanted, bending the world to his will
for pleasure or power, Kamashoka was ripe for conversion –

to reign in peace, follow the path of truth, mitigate suffering;
serve his people and country, achieve greater good as King.

Thus began his long journey to change the world
by changing himself, turning into Dhammashoka.

Life had lead him to dharma, suffering to freedom,
taught him bad can change to good, delusion to wisdom –

how the pursuit of wealth and power played their part
in resolving conflicts and dilemmas of the human heart.

IV

Ten years after his coronation Ashoka visited Sambodhi,
sought the council of the enlightened and holy.

Meeting the aged, poor and disabled, he made provisions
for their welfare. From his forest-dwelling subjects

he learnt to see the world through their eyes –
waking to his responsibility as a true leader.

Dreaming of an empire founded on peace and virtue,
on stone pillars and rocks, architectural marvels each –

imperial inscriptions carved in the people's tongue
spelled the rule of law, ahimsa and tolerance.

Edicts extolling the dignity of man and the sacredness
of life adorned popular public places.

On top of the most famous of Ashoka's pillars stood
four lions, facing outwards, symbolising self-conquest.

This is the proclamation of King Ashoka, Beloved of the Gods:

It is more than two and half years since I became a follower
of the Buddha, and over a year since I joined the Sangha –

placing my faith in the path of Dhamma.
Our subjects who never mingled with gods do so now.

Self-realization is no longer limited to a privileged few,
none is excluded from entering the kingdom of heaven.

Those living outside our protection can embrace Dhamma,
benefit from self-restraint, celebrate the gift of life.

Obey your mother and father, honour your teachers and elders,
be steadfast in your reverence for all God's creatures.

Live with integrity, respect one another. Let your actions
in the pursuit of truth and happiness be everlasting.

The poorest of the poor are now able to invest in Dhamma,
which will increase manifold and to half as much again.

It is difficult to do good to others, and he who acts
with greater good in mind accomplishes what is divine.

V

All that is born must die. Nothing that comes to be
brings permanent joy, pain and happiness are illusory.

Knowing suffering to be the key to self-awareness,
Ashoka led a life of duty, decency and selflessness.

Just as a traveller knows the real value of home,
dukkha deepened Ashoka's appreciation of bliss.

High-ranking officers were appointed across the land
to encourage his subjects to follow the path of dhamma.

From scribes and teachers to charioteers and elephant-riders,
all were enlisted in the practice of compassion:

Go among my subjects with this message of hope and peace.
As the sun banishes darkness, it will open their eyes

dulled by ignorance. Urge my people
to be patient in their search for fulfilment and prosperity,

to have faith in Dhamma and act accordingly.
It will enrich them beyond their dreams, individually.

My message must be heard by everyone,
from the most humble to the highly exalted.

Gifts are meritorious, favours are hard earned,
yet no gift or favour is greater than that of Dhamma.

From slaves and servants to parents and elders,
from friends and relatives to priests and neighbours –

Dhamma is showing consideration to all creatures,
even kings are enriched by acts of clemency.

Believing all seekers of truth to be divine messengers,
and the path to enlightenment a matter of grace than right –

Ashoka submitted himself unreservedly to his inner guide,
praying for passage to that sublime state of mind.

In the grand sweep of time, change is inevitable –
only Dhamma is eternal, keeper of all things real, spiritual.

Life's a mirror that reflects our choices,
the struggle to see the light our true measure.

VI

Atoning for the lives of thousands of Kalingans –
innocent men and women who suffered intolerable

violence, death and banishment, Ashoka felt culpable,
not only for his own unforgivable sins,

but that of his men who executed his regime of terror,
inflicted pain and injustice on brave and blameless souls.

When families are broken the spiritual foundation
of society is destroyed, leaving a trail of desolation.

Making amends for the agony of those who died
and those who survived, Ashoka vowed to do good.

He hoped with right action based on renunciation
he could atone for his past transgression.

A man of action, he valued most the rich flowering
of virtue among his subjects like the Bodhi tree spreading

its branches, putting down roots, its massive trunk centred
in the fertile soil of discrimination. He declared

there be no extolment of one's personal sect, or disparagement
of others' creeds – the foundation of civil society built

on knowing one's limits, respecting that of others,
and restraint, especially with regard to self-aggrandizement.

Those who are attached to their respective sects – from ladies
of the royal households to officers in charge of cattle and pastures –

must realize the King does not value gifts or honours
as highly as true respect for all God's creatures.

Treat all sects as you would like to be regarded by others.
Blessed are those who live in harmony with their neighbours.

The mastery of the self in doing one's duty was considered
the noblest of battles by the war-scarred Ashoka.

To such a conquest he'd devoted himself after the apocalypse
of Kalinga, his latest victories measured by the rise

of compassion in his commonwealth. He inscribed his edicts
for the benefit of his people, believing the freedom

to practice Dhamma by their subjects the highest
achievement of all who aspire to be great leaders:

Faith in the path of Dhamma is a truth that bears repetition.
Liberation is not causing harm to any of God's creation.

VII

Full twelve years after Ashoka became a follower
of the Buddha, the practice of non-violence began to flower

in his kingdom – the slaughter of animals for pleasure
or sacrifice was banished, including the daily killing of a deer

and two peacocks for the royal table. By his order
even fish in the sea, rivers and lakes were protected –

the taking of life made punishable by law—
and sanctuaries built for humans and animals.

Where medicinal herbs for healing could not be found,
they were imported for plantation. Where no vegetables,

roots or fruits grew, the land was made fit for cultivation.
Along every road, wells were dug, trees planted.

Where no roads existed they were built by royal decree.

Ashoka wanted his subjects to experience the exaltation
of a good life, not be weighed down by depravation,

adharma, intolerance, falsehood or cruelty.
His reign promised justice, peace, liberty –

the pursuit of enlightened happiness an inalienable
right. His mind hungry and fearless, thirsty and supple,

he never swerved from his dream of building heaven on earth.
Royal Dhamma-Mahamattas were appointed to travel

the length and breadth of his domain – not excluding the lands
ruled by the Greeks, Yavanas, Kambojas and Gandharas –

to implement the benign laws of his nation. They proclaimed
with the beating of drums, displays of celestial chariots,

pageants of caparisoned elephants with musicians, dancers,
fireworks and other spectacular performances –

the loftiest ideals that ever inspired a king:

Thanks to the enlightened traditions established by our King,
the sound of the drum has become the dhwani of Dhamma.

Goodness is right conduct, the abstention from taking life.
Meritorious it is to spend little, save a little, and own little.

Farmers and traders, servants and wealthy householders,
destitute and nobles, young and old, soldiers and teachers,

monks and nuns are all equal in the eyes of Dhamma,
whose practise enriches its followers beyond all measure.

VIII

Believing there is no duty more sacred than serving
and preserving life, Ashoka carved his edicts

on ornamental pillars of rock for the benefit of posterity:

This record relating to Dhamma is for generations to come
so my descendants may conform to its custom.

In the past no attention was paid to executing affairs
of the state in a timely manner. Now, *officers*

will report matters concerning my people
at any time or place, regardless of what I am doing –

whether I am with emissaries, engaged in a meeting,
in the harem, in my bed-chamber, on a promenade,

in the royal carriage or in the pleasure gardens.
The needs of my people are more important than mine.

When I issue an order, if there is a dispute or difference
of opinion regarding its interpretation, it must be brought

to my attention urgently, so justice can be served promptly.
It is my desire to discharge my debt to all living beings –

enable my subjects to live in peace,
practising self-restraint and purity of thought.

Since our visit to Sambodhi, the tree of enlightenment,
I have gone on pilgrimages, met ascetics and holy men,

bestowed gifts and gold on the destitute, ill and aged,
discussed with many the meaning of Dhamma –

it is compassion for all living creatures.
To ensure every act of ours enriches the universe

we must be free of injustice, inhumanity and corruption.
It is difficult for the rich to remain pure, avoid temptation.

No greater grace for a king to establish heaven on earth,
no success superior or sweeter than the reign of truth.

All other pleasures and pursuits pale by comparison –
not the winning of empires, wealth, glory or recognition.

IX

Knowing whatever good he wished to achieve
would be delivered by his appointed officers,

Ashoka left in writing strict instructions:
You may not grasp the extent of my intention

to deliver justice fairly and impartially,
implement the principles of Dhamma universally.

If an officer fails to do his duty owing to the following
dispositions – jealousy, anger, cruelty, hastiness,

want of perseverance, laziness or fatigue –
he does me, his King, grave injustice.

You should endeavour these failings do not restrict
your ability to deliver truth and justice.

Success lies in the absence of such limitations.
The observance of duty will produce great results.

If you fail, there will be for you neither
the attainment of heaven nor royal favour.

This record has been written that officers of the city
may strive at all times to do their duty –

so people within their charges do not suffer
from unnecessary harassment or imprisonment.

My Mahamattas, who will be neither harsh nor fierce
in temperament, but thoughtful, considerate and impartial

will tour the country to ascertain if the officers
are acting according to my instructions.

The following be respected with regard to all creatures –
non-injury, restraint, impartiality.

Such a conquest Ashoka wished to realize,
not only in his own realm, also in the territories

bordering his kingdom, as far away as where reigned
the Greek King Antiochus, and beyond his realm

in the lands of the four kings – Ptolemy, Antigonus,
Magas of Curene and Alexander of Epicurus.

X

Immersed in the service of humanity, Ashoka lived
free of encumbrances, directing the resources of his empire

to win over the waverers to the way of Dhamma:

I endeavour to be free from debt to all creatures –
all my effort is directed to such a purpose.

If I can render some happiness in this world,
enable my people to gain heaven in the next
that will be reward enough.

He kept a watchful eye on the welfare of his people,
their happiness determining his –

imagined gods associating with his subjects,
and they in turn living like divine beings.

Yet no time or place was ever a haven for the old,
even with Dhamma at the centre of its fold.

Faced with revolts, intrigues, uprisings in his kingdom,
beset with troubles in the heart of his family,

Dhammashoka's hold over his empire began to weaken
as violence ceased to be associated with his reign.

Dhamma failed to conquer all, the illusion of greatness
no more preserved by military prowess.

Ashoka was not as blessed as his grandfather,
who having excelled in his duty as king and warrior

abdicated his throne, became an ascetic,
choosing to die by slow starvation as a faithful Jaina did.

Compelled to protect his beloved empire,
even as the years began to chip away his ascendency,

the once formidable fighter could no longer
hold his world together. After thirty-seven years as emperor,

disappointed, disillusioned, divested of his mighty power
acquired at a cost no longer imaginable, in the end

Ashoka was left with half a fruit – a bitter-sweet amla or
was it a mango? The Ashokavadana exaggerates.

Truth is the majesty of Ashoka's dream, his supreme
legacy and estate, the reign of Dhamma, perished with him.

Dramatic indeed the decline and dissolution
of the Mauryan empire after the death of Ashoka.

NOTES

In The Beginning: The image of the inverted tree is a representation of the divine. In Hinduism, at the time of Creation, the Divine consciousness manifested itself as Shunyākāsha, which translates to nothing or zero (Shunya) and sky (Ākāsha). It was not 'nothingness' as everything existed in a latent state of potentiality.

In the Jagannath Temple: *Jagannath swami, prabhu antarjyami* ... a prayer to Lord Jagannath, acknowledged as the Lord of the universe.

Belshazzar's Feast: *Do not despair, one was saved; do not presume, one was damned* refers to a quote from Samuel Beckett's *Waiting for Godot*. The original source is Saint Augustine. *The Unbearable Lightness of Being* is the title of Milan Kundera's 1984 novel.

The Seagull: Poem inspired by a conversation overheard between two members of the audience after seeing Anton Chekhov's play, *The Seagull*.

City Slickers: Written after the Bishopsgate bombing, City of London, by the Irish Republican Army on 24 April 1993.

Batchelors Soup: The title of the poem refers to a brand of instant soups available in the UK.

To Be a Beginner: Carpe diem: Phrase from a Latin poem by Horace, where *Carpe diem quam minimum credula postero* translates to 'Seize the day, putting as little trust as possible in the next (day)'. As the future is unforeseen, the quote implies one should scale back one's hopes and live in the present. The phrase is usually interpreted in the light of Horace's Epicurean background. In Hindu thought the ability to take charge of one's fate hinges on self-realization by living a 'good' life every moment.

Highgate Cemetery: *Of those immortal dead who live again/ in minds made better by their presence* – epitaph on George Eliot's tomb in Highgate Cemetery, London.

Loneliness: *The road not taken* from Robert Frost's poem is a metaphor for life – the choices we make in a crisis, the connection between free will and fate.

Learning: *To keep awake ... an original relation with the universe* is a quote from Ralph Waldo Emerson's 1836 essay, 'Nature'.

What Might Have Been: Khurshid, wife of the poet Keki Daruwalla, died a week after going into a coma as a result of a paramedic van hitting their car while the family, just arrived from India, was travelling from the airport to their daughter's home in America.

Bori Notesz: In November 1944, near the Hungarian town of Abda, Radnóti was shot, along with twenty-one other crippled and emaciated captives, while being forced-marched towards Germany during the liberation of the Balkans. His body was exhumed from a ditch after the war, and identified from the notebook (*Bori Notesz*) of poems in his raincoat pocket. I am indebted to various translations of *Camp Notebook* in the writing of this poem and in capturing Radnóti 'voice' as reflected in the *Notebook*.

Life? Or Theatre?: Poem inspired by the work of Charlotte Salomon (1917–43) at a Royal Academy of Arts, London, exhibition, *Life? or Theatre? A Play with Music*. In 1943, aged twenty-six, the artist was deported from France with her Austrian–Jewish husband to Auschwitz. They arrived on 10 October, but no record exists of Salomon's death.

Shringara: Shringara is one of the nine rasas, usually translated to as erotic or romantic love. The theory of rasa is the foundation of classical Indian art, including theatre, music, dance, poetry, sculpture. Much of traditional Indian art deals with the relationship between a man and a woman, the primary emotion generated being shringara. The relationship between lover and beloved is also a metaphor for the relationship between the individual and the Divine. In classical Indian painting and sculpture, the shringara rasa is represented by a woman getting ready, putting on make-up, sitting or standing in front of a mirror, facing herself, preparing for a lover, her life. In my poem, shringara refers to all kinds of preparation we make for Life itself. The idea of being prepared also reminds me of Shakespeare's '*ripeness is all*' (*King Lear*, Act 5, Scene 2, 'Men must endure/ Their going hence even as their coming hither. / Ripeness is all.').

Italian Prayer: *Chiesa d'Oro*: Church of Gold.

Black Swans: In his book, *The Black Swan*, Nassim Nicholas Taleb refers to an event with rarity, extreme impact, and retrospective predictability as a Black Swan. According to Taleb, 'a small number of Black Swans explain almost everything in our world, from the success of ideas and religions, to the dynamics of historical events, to elements of our own personal lives.'

It: Poem based on the edition of Inger Christensen's *it*, published by Carcanet in 2007, translated by Susanna Nied, who won the 2005 PEN Translation Fund Award.

What Does It Mean?: Poem inspired by a major retrospective of Damien Hirst's work held in the Tate Modern, London, in 2012.

Time Uncovering Truth: Poem based on news reports when Silvio Berlusconi was Italy's prime minister. His staff altered a reproduction of a famous eighteenth-century painting by Giambattista Tiepolo to cover an exposed breast on full display in the press room at the Palazzo Chigi, the prime minister's palace.

Saxophone Colossus: A tribute to the jazz musician Sonny Rollins (tenor saxophone), based on a concert at The Barbican Hall, London, on 14 November 2009. His accompanists were Clifton Anderson (trombone), Bobby Broom (guitar), Bob Cranshaw (bass), Kobie Watkins (drums), and Victor Y. See Yuen (percussion). *Tenor Madness* and *Saxophone Colossus* are among Rollins' best known jazz recordings.

Wonder Of The Age: Poem inspired by an exhibition at the British Library, *Mughal India: Art, Culture and Empire*. Having seen

M.F. Husain: Master of Modern Indian Painting at the Victoria & Albert Museum, I dedicate my poem to the masters of Indian painting.

Painter Of Gods: Patta-chitra is a unique form of painting in Odisha. Patta refers to the canvas used in such paintings (chitra). The Puri patta-chitras were traditionally devoted to the depiction of the Trinity – Lord Jagannath with his brother Balabhadra and sister, Subhadra. Today's patta-chitras include various deities in the Hindu pantheon.

Eurydice's Story: When Orpheus returned to Thrace without Eurydice, he was so inconsolable he would have nothing to do with other women. The outraged Thracian women tore him to pieces in a bacchanalian revel. The fragments of his body were collected by the Muses and buried at the feet of Mount Olympus. Orpheus's head, which had been tossed into the river Hebrus, was carried into the sea and floated ashore on to the island of Lesbos, becoming the famous Oracle.

Savitri chose her husband Satyavan. So firm was her devotion to him that when he died she asked Yama, the Lord of Death, for the gift of his life. Yama offered Savitri any boon except the life of her husband. She asked for the restoration of her father-in-law's eyesight and his throne, sons for herself and a life in all its fullness. When Yama granted all her wishes, she reminded him she needed her husband to fulfil her wishes. Impressed with her intelligence and love for her husband, he is supposed to have released Satyavan to return with Savitri. Indian wives continue to observe a day in memory of Sati Savitri, the pure one.

The Scream: Poem inspired by three different experiences. In August 2012, I was reading about the origin of Edvard Munch's *The Scream*, where he wrote: 'One evening I was walking along a road – with the fjord and the town below on the other side. I was sick and tired – I stood for some time looking across the fjord – The sun was setting – the clouds were turning red – like blood. I felt as if a scream was going through nature – I thought I heard a scream. I painted the picture – painted the clouds like real blood – The colours were screaming.'

At the time I was also reading Rilke's poems. On 19 January 1912, standing on the bastions of Castle Duino on the Adriatic (home of his admirer and friend, Princess Marie von Thurn und Taxis-Hohenlohe) while the wind howled around him, Rainer Maria Rilke (4 December 1875 – 29 December 1926) heard a voice: 'Who, if I cried out, would hear me among the ranks of the angels?' Then on Armistice Day 2012, I was in my kitchen, facing the window overlooking Highgate Wood, admiring the sunset. When I switched on the radio, the news was all about war and death. In a moment of epiphany, the history of suffering flashed in front of me. An inaudible cry escaped my lips.

Nirbhaya: Poem inspired by the death of Jyoti Singh Pandey who was gang-raped in a bus in Delhi on 16 December 2012. According to Indian law, as she was raped, her name was not publicly disclosed, even after her death. The media called the twenty-three-year-old, Nirbhaya, the fearless one. It was her father, Badrinath Singh, who revealed her name. He wanted the world to know who she was.

Ashoka: In August 2011, London witnessed its worst riots in recent history. It stirred memories among the older generation in the UK of their experiences during the Blitz. The riots manifested a breakdown of moral values in society, a collective failure of leadership, which made me wonder: what makes a true leader? I was reading about Ashoka, the Indian king, who ascended the throne of the Mauryas in 269–268 BC. After his accession, Ashoka set out to complete his occupation of the Indian subcontinent by invading the then fiercely independent state of Kalinga, modern-day Odisha, where I was born. The savage war that followed brought about a radical change in Ashoka's attitude to war and kingship. He embraced Dhamma (the Prakrit form of the Sanskrit word Dharma), the virtuous path that guides the follower through a life of duty, selflessness, decency, good conduct. While the concept of dharma existed in all religions in India, Ashoka turned to Buddhism, which by the time of his reign had manifested itself as a socio-intellectual movement. Unlike the Buddha, Ashoka did not seek nirvana. Nor was he like Arjuna, the main protagonist of the Mahabharata, despondent in the face of battle. An astute soldier, Ashoka was quick to see the limits of violence. His achievement lay in transforming dharma, the highest form of social responsibility, into state policy. Ashoka became a true leader through the strength of his ideas. For Ashoka to adopt ahimsa as state policy in the third century BC was inspirational. He renounced war, reaching out instead to his subjects to address their concerns. He encouraged religious freedom, self-knowledge, the need for leaders and citizens to listen to each other and debate ideas. He made a deep commitment to family values, education, health, rule of law and the idea of happiness. Not much is known of his life towards the end of his reign. Ashoka did not abdicate nor was he deposed. Yet, within fifty years after his death, the Mauryan dynasty collapsed.

ACKNOWLEDGEMENTS

My thanks to the editors of the following publications in which most of the poems in this selection first appeared, sometimes in earlier versions:

Bengal Lights and *Six Seasons Review* in **Bangladesh**

Ariel, *The Dance of the Peacock: An Anthology of English Poetry from India* (2013), *The Toronto Review*, *The Toronto Review of Contemporary Writing Abroad* and *The Toronto South Asian Review* in **Canada**

World Poetry Yearbook 2013 and 2014 co-edited by Dr Choi Lai Sheung and Dr Zhang Zhi and *The World Poets Quarterly* in **China**

Paris/ Atlantic and *The French Literary Review* in **France**

Asia Literary Review in **Hong Kong**

An Anthology of Modern Poetry edited by Pranab Bandyopadhyay (1977), *By Word, Celebrating Creativity* (Hyderabad Literary Festival, 2010), *Chandrabhaga*, *Commonwealth Quarterly*, *ELT Forum Journal of English Studies*, *Home Thoughts: Poetry of the British Indian Diaspora* edited by Usha Kishore and Jaydeep Sarangi (2016), *Hundred Indian Poets* edited by Pranab Bandyopadhyay (1977), *Illuminati: A Transnational Journal of Literature, Language and Culture Studies*, *Imprint*, *India in Verse* edited by Antara Dev Sen (2011), *India International Centre Quarterly*, *Indian Association for Commonwealth Literature and Language Studies' Souvenir Issue*, *Indian English Women Poets* edited by Anisur Rahman and Ameena Kazi Ansari (2009), *Indian Journal of Postcolonial Literatures*, *Indian Literature*, *Indian Literary Review*, *Indian National Journal of English Language and Literatures*, *Indian Verse*, *In Their Own Voice: The Penguin Anthology of Contemporary Indian Women Poets* edited by Dr Arlene R.K. Zide (1993), *Journal of Children's Literature*, *Journal of the Indian P.E.N.*, *Journal of Indian Writing in English*, *Journal of Literature and Aesthetics*, *Kavi India*, *Kavya Bharati*, *Kritya*, *Labyrinth: The Literary Journal of Post-Modernism*, *Modern Poetry*, *New Quest*, *Objet-d'-Art*, *Panorama Literaria*, *Poet*, *Poetry Chain*, *Poetry Chronicle*, *Poets Travelogue: The Grand Indian Express* edited by Anand Kumar (2016), *Poiesis*, *Poesie India International*, *Prosopisia*, *Re-Markings*, *Roots and Wings: An Anthology of Indian Women Writing in English* edited by Annie George and Sandhya S.N. (2011), *Samyukta: A Journal of Women's Studies*, *Shakti*, *Shaping Minds: Multicultural Literature* edited by Nibir K. Ghosh (2010), *The Bombay Review*, *The HarperCollins Book of English Poetry* edited by Sudeep Sen (2012), *The Humanities Review*, *The ICFAI University Journal of Commonwealth Literature*, *The Illustrated Weekly Of India*, *The IUP Journal of Commonwealth Literature*, *The Journal of the Poetry Society*, *The Little Magazine*, *The Miscellany*, *The Phoenix*, *The Ravenshavian*, *The Second Genesis: An Anthology of Contemporary World Poetry* edited by Anuraag Sharma (2014), *To Catch a Poem* edited by Anju Makhija and Jane Bhandari (2014), *Vortex*, *We Speak in Changing Languages: Indian Woman Poets 1990-2007* edited by E.V. Ramakrishnan and Anju Makhija (2009), *Wings over the Mahanadi: Eight Odia-English Poets* edited by Manu Dash (2014) and *Youth Times* in **India**

Seeing the Wood and the Trees edited by Rosemarie Rowley and John Haughton (2003) in **Ireland**

Private Photo Review and *Private International Photo Review* in **Italy**

Selected Poems of the United Kingdom edited by Patricia Oxley (2000) in **Nepal**

JAAM and *Poetry New Zealand* in **New Zealand**

Carapace in **South Africa**

The Istanbul Review in **Turkey**

Acumen, *Aesthetica: A Review of Contemporary Artists*, *A Glass of New Made Wine* edited by W. Görtschacher and G. Pursglove (1999),

Agenda, *Ambit*, *Artrage*, *Chapman*, *Coffee House Poetry*, *Confluence*, *Connections: The Literary Scene In The South*, *Critical Quarterly*, *Critical Survey*, *Delhi London Poetry Quarterly*, *Dream Catcher*, *Edinburgh Review*, *Envoi*, *Exile*, *Exiled Ink!*, *Feminist Arts News*, *Fire*, *First Sixty: The Acumen Anthology* edited by Patricia Oxley (25th Anniversary Issue, 2010), *Guardian Poem of the Week* edited by Carol Rumens (26 September 2011), *Home: An Anthology* edited by Kathleen McPhilemy (2000), *Images of Women: An Anthology of Poetry by Contemporary Women Poets* edited by Myra Schneider and Dilys Wood (2006), *In the Company of Poets* edited by John Rety (2003), *Into the Further Reaches* edited by Jay Ramsay (2007), *Iota Poetry Quarterly*, *Journal of Orissa Society, UK* (2009), *Journal of Postcolonial Writing*, *Littoral*, *London Magazine*, *Masala: Poems from India, Bangladesh, Pakistan and Sri Lanka* chosen by Debjani Chatterjee (2005), *Mslexia*, *Moving Beyond Boundaries: International Dimensions of Black Women's Writing* edited by Carole Boyce Davies and 'Molara Ogundipe-Leslie (1994), *Moving Worlds: A Journal of Transcultural Writings*, *Never Bury Poetry*, *New Hope International*, *New Moon Rises* edited by Sean Woodward (1993), *New Poetry* (*Asian Women Writers Collective*, 1994), *New Soundings in Postcolonial Writing: Critical and Creative Contours* edited by Janet Wilson and Chris Ringrose (2016), *New Welsh Review*, *Not Only the Dark: 160 Poems on the Theme of Survival* edited by Jo Field and Nicky Gould (2011), *Only Connect* edited by Gail Ashton and Jan Fortune-Wood (2007), *Orbis: Quarterly International Literary Journal*, *Other Poetry*, *Out of Bounds: British Black and Asian Poets* edited by Jackie Kay, James Proctor and Gemma Robinson (2012), *Oxford Quarterly Review*, *Oxford Today*, *Pennine Platform*, *Pentacle Magazine*, *Philosophy Now*, *Planet – The Welsh Internationalist*, *Plant Care: A Festschrift for Mimi Khalvati* edited by E.A. Markham (2004), *Poems on the Buses* (London, 1992), *Poetry London Newsletter*, *Poetry Monthly*, *Poetry Nottingham International*, *Poetry Now*, *Poetry Postcard Quarterly*, *Poetry Review*, *Poetry Street*, *Poetry Today*, *PN Review*, *Pulsar Poetry Magazine*, *Red: Contemporary Black British Poetry* edited by Kwame Dawes (2010), *Read On ...2* (Asian Women Writers Collective), *SCINTILLA*, *Seam*, *Sheffield Thursday*, *Society Today*, *Soul Feathers: An Anthology to Aid the Work of Macmillan Cancer Support* edited by Ronnie Goodyer and Annie Morgan (2011), *South Asian Diaspora Literature and Arts Archive*, *Spokes Poetry Magazine*, *Thumbscrew*, *Torriano Nights: A Festschrift for John Rety* edited by Phil Poole (2009), *The Arcadian*, *The Bloodaxe Book of Contemporary Indian Poets* edited by Jeet Thayil (2008), *The Book of Love and Loss* edited by R.V. Bailey and June Hall (2014), *The Bound Spiral*, *The Frogmore Papers*, *The Interpreter's House*, *The New Welsh Review*, *The New Writer*, *The Poet's Quest For God: 21st Century Poems of Faith, Doubt and Wonder* edited by Fr Oliver Brennan and Todd Swift (2016), *The Redbeck Anthology of British South Asian Poetry* edited by Debjani Chatterjee (2000), *The Rialto*, *The Swansea Review*, *The Warwick Review*, *The Works 4* edited by Pie Corbett and Gaby Morgan (2005), *Urthona: A Journal of Buddhism and the Arts*, *Velocity: the Best of Apples and Snakes* (2003), *Wasafiri*, *Weyfarers*, *Word Masala Award Winners 2015* edited by Yogesh Patel, *World Poetry Day* (Tongues and Grooves in conjunction with the BBC and Portsmouth University screened 'Italian Prayer' on the Big Screen in Guildhall Square, Portsmouth, on 21 March 2012) and *World Literature Written in English* in the **UK**.

Cimarron Review, *College Poetry Review*, *Contemporary Indian Poetry* edited by Kaiser Haq (1990), *Give the Sea Change and It Shall Change: An Anthology of Indian Poetry in English* (1951-2005) edited by Jeet Thayil (2005), *Hurricane Alice*, *Journal of South Asian Literature* (Michigan State University), *Language for a New Century: Contemporary Poetry from the Middle East, Asia and Beyond* edited by Tina Chang, Nathalie Handal and Ravi Shankar (2008), *Lips, Fingertips, and the Future of English* by Mark Abley (2008), *Live Life: The Daydreamer's Journal: An International Anthology of Short Stories and Poetry for Charity* (2012), *Mother Earth International*, *South Asian Review*, *United Poets Laureate International* and *Unmapped: The Indian Poetry Issue* edited by Sudeep Sen (2009) in the **USA**.

I am grateful to the editors of websites where my poems featured. They include: Acumen, Agenda, And Other Poems, Asia Literary Review, Arvon Foundation, CAESURAE, Carapace, Cerebration, Dimdima, Eyewear, Guardian Poem Of The Week, Jazzwise Magazine, Kalakahani, Kritya, Lakeview International Journal of Literature and Arts, London Grip, Message in a Bottle, Morphrog, Muse India, Nth Position, Poets of London, Poetry Pacific, Postcolonial Text, Private Photo Review, Skylark Publications, Sulekha, The Brown Critique, The Criterion, The International Literary Quarterly Inc, The Poetry Shed, The World Poets Quarterly and Varnamala.

In addition to the editors and reviewers for their critical insights, I would like to thank those who have, over the years, read my poems, provided constructive feedback. They include Mark Abley, R.V. Bailey, Carole Baldock, John Bayley, Anne Beer, Jaysinh Birjépatil, Alison Brackenbury, Martyn Crucefix, Kamala Das, Keki Daruwalla, Ketaki Kushari Dyson, Nissim Ezekiel, Lakshmi Holmström, Lakshmi Kannan, Mimi Khalvati, Lance Lee, Paul Love, Anna Sujatha Mathai, Anita Money, Alastair Niven, Patricia and William Oxley, Bibhu Padhi, Ayyappa Paniker, Rajagopal Parthasarathy, Deba Patnaik, Peter Porter, Carol Rumens, K. Satchidanandan, Cecile Sandten, Carole Satyamurti, Penelope Shuttle, Amritjit Singh, K. Srilata, Anne Stevenson, Seán Street, George Szirtes, M.L.H.L. Weaver, and Janet Wilson. My indebtedness to the many poets, writers, thinkers, artists, philosophers, scientists, historians, friends, family and others who shaped my thought, work and life cannot be fully or individually acknowledged. Each poem is a tribute.

A world of thanks with my gratitude to HarperCollins India, especially Shantanu Ray Chaudhuri. Special thanks to my brother, Sanjay Acharya, for the cover photograph. Without the love and support of my family, none of this would have been possible.

ALSO BY SHANTA ACHARYA

POETRY

Dreams That Spell The Light

Shringara

Looking In, Looking Out

Numbering Our Days' Illusions

Not This, Not That

CD

Somewhere, Something: Shanta Acharya reading a selection of her poems

STUDIES IN AMERICAN LITERATURE

The Influence of Indian Thought on Ralph Waldo Emerson

FICTION

A World Elsewhere

ASSET MANAGEMENT

Endowment Asset Management: Investment Strategies in Oxford and Cambridge (with Elroy Dimson)

Asset Management: Equities Demystified

Investing In India

www.shantaacharya.com